LYNDA FIELD'S

More Than
60 WAYS
TO MAKE
YOUR LIFE
AMAZING

A Complete Guide for Women

ELEMENT

Shaftesbury, Dorset • Boston, Massachusetts
Melbourne, Victoria

© Element Books Limited 2000
Text © Lynda Field 2000

First published in the UK in 2000 by
Element Books Limited
Shaftesbury, Dorset SP7 8BP

Published in the USA in 2000 by
Element Books, Inc.
160 North Washington Street
Boston, MA 02114

Published in Australia in 2000 by
Element Books and distributed
by Penguin Australia Limited
487 Maroondah Highway, Ringwood,
Victoria 3134

Cover design by Prospero-Digital
Designed and typeset by Bournemouth Colour Press
Printed and bound in Great Britain by
J W Arrowsmith Ltd, Bristol

British Library Cataloguing in Publication
data available

Library of Congress Cataloging in Publication
data available

ISBN 1 86204 835 5

Contents

Dedicated to all women, everywhere

Preface

Sisters are doing it for themselves ...

Annie Lennox

Our life is a precious gift, miraculous and amazing, but we are not always able to appreciate this miracle fully.

The power of our womanhood brings together the unique and amazing gifts of our gender: to be resourceful and flexible; to overcome obstacles and face our challenges with humour and perseverance; to show patience and have endurance; to love and appreciate ourselves and all those around us; to reach our true potential; to reach for the stars; to live our dreams.

But life is not always easy and when we face obstacles and difficulties it can be hard to stay positive, upbeat and decisive. *More Than 60 Ways to Make Your Life Amazing* reminds all women everywhere that we always have the personal strength and power to surmount our problems. Whether you are feeling overstretched and muddled; low in confidence; unhappy with your body image; too tired for sex; disappointed in love; powerless and victimized; or every one of these things *and more*, take heart you can change all of this!

Let this book be a constant reminder to you that you have the power to change yourself and your circumstances. Twenty-first-century woman has the awareness, capacity and power to make a success of all aspects of her life. She can indeed *have it all* and make her life truly amazing!

Lynda Field

Introduction

You are a strong and powerful woman. You are thoughtful, intuitive, resilient, sensitive and creative, and when you bring all of these qualities together you feel confident, alive, energetic, successful, assertive and empowered and your life becomes a dynamic and amazing experience.

Perhaps you don't feel like a strong and powerful woman. What do you see when you look at yourself? Be honest here. What changes would you like to make to improve the quality of your life? Are you getting what you want? Do you know how to be assertive and risk-taking? Are you reaching your potential and living your dreams? Is your life an exciting experience? If not, then why not? How can you find the special and individual help you may need to resolve your very own personal problems?

Recently, as I stood at the self-help shelves of a popular bookshop, the woman next to me turned to me saying, 'There are so many books here, how do I know which one will be able to help me? It's all so confusing.' When we have a personal problem we need to know *exactly* what we can do about it; we need specific answers to specific problems and the shelves heaving with self-help manuals can be intimidating and unhelpful. And so, when I was asked to write a companion volume to *60 Ways to Feel Amazing* I decided to address the actual problems and issues that women face daily and to make this book really user-friendly. I have designed the Power Matrix which lists the specific problems which many women face along with the relevant chapters which show how to deal with the problem. So, for example, if you were having trouble with your relationships you could look through the matrix until you found *Difficulties with Relationships* and then turn to the relevant chapters: *you would not have to read the whole book to find your solution!*

Look through the matrix which follows on the next pages. Alongside each problem are the numbers of the key chapters which will help you to find your solution. Each chapter explains how it will help you and then takes you through your own personal techniques for change, which I have called workouts. At the end of each chapter is a summary of the essential points, the Key Power Points, and these will help you to remain focused. Use this book as you would use a personal trainer: it will guide you to the specific workouts you need and will provide encouragement and support throughout.

Go ahead: face your challenges, reclaim your power and bring excitement to your days. Make your life amazing!

For up-to-date news on personal development, tips for success, newsletters, online coaching and much much more please visit my website at:
www.lyndafield.com

Power Matrix

Problem	Key chapters
Stress	2, 3, 6, 18
Unable to trust others	11, 17, 18, 19
Uncomfortable with your sexuality	8, 12
You have reached your limit	2, 5, 6, 8
Men usually make decisions for you	1, 7, 10
Feeling powerless	1, 3, 4, 6, 11, 19, 20
Overtired	2, 3
Low in self-esteem and confidence	1, 3, 4, 7, 8, 10, 20
Worry about body shape	4, 6, 8, 12
Dissatisfaction with life	1, 3, 5, 6, 8, 17, 20
Can't trust yourself	1, 11, 16, 18,
Difficulties with relationships	4, 7, 9, 13
Always too much to do	2, 3, 6
Depression	4, 5, 6, 8, 14, 18, 19
Your intimate relationship has lost its sparkle	1, 7, 12, 13, 18
Craving peace and calm	2, 6, 20
Wanting someone to change	4, 7, 9
Poor body image	4, 8, 12
Feeling angry	2, 14, 20
Can't stop and relax	2, 3, 6
Life is miserable	1, 2, 6, 17
You are trying to change a man	7, 9, 16
Sexual inexperience	12
Oversensitivity and vulnerability	5, 6, 10, 11, 14, 17, 18, 19, 20
Hard to take action	3, 6, 8, 10, 11, 14, 18

Your partner doesn't understand you	7, 9, 10, 13
Feeling that you are not a 'good enough' mother	4, 7, 11, 15
Self hate	6, 7, 8, 11, 12, 14, 16
Fear of change	4, 8, 11, 17, 19, 20
Need to be uplifted	6, 17, 18, 19, 20
In an abusive relationship	7, 8, 16, 18, 19
Too tired for sex	3, 12, 20
Life is disappointing	1, 2, 5, 18
Feeling victimized by your family	1, 4, 7, 8, 9, 13, 15
An intimate relationship has ended badly	7, 10, 11, 12, 13
Your world has fallen apart	6, 8, 18, 19, 20
Feelings of guilt and shame	11, 14, 15, 16, 17, 20
Can't make decisions	1, 4, 7, 10
Insecurity	1, 4, 5, 6, 8, 11, 14, 15, 19
You need to change something in your life	1, 8, 9, 10, 11, 20
Life is dull	2, 6, 8, 17, 18
Difficulties in maintaining intimate personal relationships	4, 6, 7, 9, 12, 13, 17
Feeling too old to be noticed	1, 8, 12
Lack of success	1, 4, 18, 19
Everything is going wrong	5, 6, 8, 9, 14, 19, 20
You feel like a victim	1, 4, 8, 20
Lack of sexual desire	12, 20
Feeling muddled and out of control	1, 2, 3, 8

You

1 Being a Winner

I'm a reminder that anything in life is possible, whenever you think you can't, think of me and know that you can.

Zoe Koplowitz

Zoe Koplowitz is a 50-year-old diabetic, multiple sclerosis sufferer who crossed the 1999 London marathon finishing line 30 hours after starting the race. Zoe completed the 26-mile race on a pair of purple crutches, 28 hours after the winner and is now in training for the New York marathon.

- Whenever you find it hard to make decisions.
- If you find it difficult to relate to being a winner.
- If you feel like a victim in any area of your life.
- When you feel invisible.
- If your life is a disappointment.
- If you always seem to miss out on being successful.
- If you are inclined to let a man make decisions for you.
- When it feels that life is passing you by.

Sports psychology tells us that winning has as much to do with mental toughness as ability. Research suggests that up to 70 per cent of our daily thoughts are negative as opposed to positive: on a bad day I'm sure this figure could be even higher! But we can change this. In the same way that top sports people use mental agility to succeed, we can use it in everyday life to create winning situations.

Whilst negative thinking is a major obstacle to success we also need to be aware that many women face an added complication. As a rule, most women have not been taught to expect to be a winner, or even to want to win. However, life expectations are changing for women as girl power and woman power become acceptable concepts. Gone are the days when the little lady automatically took a submissive back seat on the home, work or relationships front. Although times are changing, many women still suffer from the after-effects of a childhood where the term 'winning' was more closely associated with the boys of the family than the girls. When we feel ambivalent about being a winner in life it's important for us to examine these mixed feelings or they will always hold us back from success.

As Zoe Koplowitz so brilliantly demonstrates, winning is not always about being first, but it *is* about always giving our absolute best in any situation. You will feel like a winner when you are striving to reach your potential; you will feel successful and confident.

HOW TO BE A WINNER

Being a winner may mean changing your thoughts and visions about yourself. The first two workouts show you how to use affirmations and visualizations to overcome negative self-beliefs and support a positive self-image. Unsuccessful people are always disappointed and are very poor decision-makers. Workout 3 introduces a brilliant strategy to improve your decision-making skills. Workout 4 lists a number of techniques which will help you to create winning ways.

1 Affirming Your Success

Your imagination is so powerful that if you fill your mind with negative thoughts about yourself you will surely become the loser you believe that you are. Watch your thoughts: negative self-beliefs will always stop your success. Become aware of your thoughts and when you find yourself thinking or saying something negative about yourself – *stop!* Replace the negativity with positive thoughts; this is how sports psychology works to create winners! Make the following affirmations:

AFFIRMATIONS: *I deserve success.*
I am a winner.
I believe in myself.

Say, sing, shout, think, write these affirmations as much as you can until you really begin to believe them.

2 Visualizing Your Success
You can use your imagination to reinforce your affirmations.

Find a comfortable place, close your eyes and relax. Follow your breathing until you feel deeply relaxed and then *see* your success in action. Picture the scene that you would like to create. See yourself being successful ... at work, at home, in a relationship, in a creative capacity ... wherever it is that you would like to be a winner. Visualize yourself succeeding – you look so confident and relaxed. Really feel what it is like to be a success. See people treating you with the respect that you deserve. Make the vision as real as you can: see and hear the whole thing in glorious colour, create the sound effects, taste the reality of your success. When you are ready let your thoughts return, open your eyes and come back into the room.

If you have negative thoughts when you are visualizing, just let them go. This technique is very powerful and in fact is one that we use all the time, but often in a negative way to support negative beliefs about ourselves. Have you ever thought that you would like to try something and then quickly decided not to bother because you wouldn't be able to do it? What has happened here is that you used a negative affirmation – a belief that 'I can't do that' which was supported by a negative visualization, when in your imagination you saw yourself failing. So you see we use these techniques all the time. Why not use them to create positivity and success?

3 Making Decisions

Are you disappointed by life? Are you a person who makes things happen or do things just keep happening to you?

If you feel like a victim of circumstance then you have lost your natural ability to create new directions for yourself. Take heart, it is easy to turn this situation around: you only need to learn to make decisions and *then act on them!*

How do you feel about making decisions? Would you describe your decision making powers as:

- Good
- Not so good
- Poor
- Can't decide?

Before you can make a decision you need to know what your goal is. If you don't have a goal you can never reach it. If you don't know where you are going you will never know when you arrive. You can't be a success if you don't know what you are trying to achieve. You cannot act if you can't decide how to act, and you can't make a decision unless you know what you intend to happen. Although this might sound obvious it does provide a key to taking charge of your life. One way to overcome all this indecision is to use IDA. IDA is a simple formula which you can use whenever you are uncertain about what to decide and therefore how to act. IDA represents the following process:

INTENTION → DECISION → ACTION

To discover your intention ask yourself this question: 'What do I want to happen?' Write down your answers because this gives your thoughts more power. (Sometimes women find it unusual to put their needs first in this way. If you do, just overcome your natural timidity and *do it anyway*.) Now decide how you need to change your behaviour in order to reach your goal. Again, write down your answers and any possible difficulties you might face and how you plan to overcome them. Now, taking everything into account ... *Act!* Just do it! Take the first step and all the rest will follow. You *can* make decisions. Prove it to yourself and there will be no stopping your progress and success!

4 Creating Winning Ways

SMILE
Feelgood chemicals are released into the body within ten seconds of smiling; even if you don't really feel happy this process still works! As you approach an important meeting, a difficult situation, even a tricky phone call, just smile, it could make all the difference.

MAKE A SUCCESS LIST
Lift yourself out of negative thinking by making a success list. Maybe things don't look so good at the moment, but

what sort of achievements have you already accomplished in your life? Write down *everything* you have been successful at. Include all areas of your life: work, leisure, relationships. Write down everything that is meaningful to you, even if it wouldn't be to anyone else. At first your list might be very small as you struggle to think of things, but the more you write the more you will remember. What about coming first in the three-legged race on Sports Day? Do you remember learning to ride a bike? You will certainly remember having a baby! How about your first date? Your first job? Passing your driving test? You see, the list goes on and on. Go back as far as you can and make a fun thing of it. Get a really big piece of paper and keep adding to the list. Memories of success will change your mood. Look at your list, what an incredible set of experiences. You see, you aren't powerless, helpless and indecisive after all – *you are a success!*

KNOW YOURSELF

Sometimes we lose confidence in our ability to be successful because we have (temporarily) lost sight of our true selves. Perhaps we have been fulfilling other people's wishes and needs. Reclaim yourself. Find out where *you* are at and what makes *you* really tick by completing the following statements:

- I most enjoy …
- My deepest desire is to …
- If only I could …
- My secret wish is to …
- My greatest regret is …
- Tomorrow I will change the way I …

When you are feeling in control of your life, making things happen and giving of your very best then you are a winner.

Your success or lack of it is a feeling and cannot be compared with that of others. Whenever negativity strikes, strike back with positive affirmations and visions: you don't have to fall into a negative downward spiral. Believe in yourself; trust your decision-making powers and discover what you really want from your life – then go out and get it! Learn how to create winning ways and stay in a positive winning cycle. Smile and the world will smile with you. Everyone loves a winner!

KEY POWER POINTS

These key points are here to remind you of why you are doing your *Being a Winner* workouts. Refer to this list for constant encouragement and support. Reclaim the power that is yours!

1 Anything in life is possible: whenever you think that you can't, know that you can.
2 Winning has as much to do with mental toughness as it has with ability.
3 As a rule, most women have not been taught to expect to be a winner or even to want to win. We need to change these thought patterns.
4 Winning is not always about being first, it is about always giving your best and striving to reach your potential.
5 Your imagination is so powerful that if you fill your mind with negative thoughts and pictures about yourself you will surely become the loser that you believe you are.
6 When you can't make a decision, answer this all-important question: 'What do I want to happen?' The rest will follow.

You

7   Smile, feel good and the world will smile with you!
8   Know yourself and trust your judgement: you are a successful and powerful woman – just believe it!
9   Create winning ways and stay in a positive cycle: everyone loves a winner.

2 De-stressing Your Life

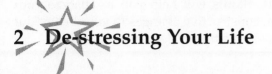

The fight-or-flight syndrome steps up the adrenaline and the release of hormones; all of your body and mind are gripped by a stress reaction. How you deal with it, whether you master it or not, can affect your life, career, health and wellbeing.

Doe Lang

- When you just want to scream!
- Whenever you feel that you have reached your limit.
- If your life is full of worry.
- When you just can't stop and relax.
- If you feel full of angry energy.
- Whenever you can't find a smile in your pocket.

If you see a situation or a person as threatening, your mind, body, spirit and emotions will register stress. But stress is in the eye of the beholder; nothing is intrinsically stressful. This may be hard to believe but it is true. By changing the way you see negative situations you can de-stress your life.

We all need a certain amount of buzz in our lives or things become flat and disinteresting. The feeling of being stretched beyond our normal limits can sometimes be exhilarating (yes, I *can* take on that new project) whereas at other times it's all just too much and we are overcome with tension and fear (I'll never do it, it's beyond me). A certain amount of stress encourages us to develop and grow, to achieve and be successful and to overcome the challenges that we meet each day. However too much stress can cause exhaustion, lethargy and eventually illness.

The following workouts will help you to analyze your stressors and make constructive changes in your behaviour and will also offer simple tips to defuse your feelings.

HOW TO DE-STRESS YOUR LIFE

The first workout will help you to focus on your own stress situations and will show you the most effective way to deal with them. The next four workouts offer simple and effective ways to deal with the build-up of tension that we all experience during our everyday life.

1 Identifying and Eliminating Unnecessary Stressors

Make a list of all the things that are negatively stressful to you. Think carefully about each stressor. Can you *let go* of it, *change* it or *accept* it in some way? Make a table like the example shown below and discover how this constructive approach can help you to eliminate unnecessary stress in your life.

Stressor	Let go	Change	Accept	Consequences
EXAMPLE 1 I always feel lethargic.		Cut down on alcohol and junk food. Eat healthily and take more exercise.		Feeling better. Looking better. Feeling more in control. Increased self-respect.
EXAMPLE 2 I'm always looking for a man to make my life complete.	Do without an intimate relationship for a while. Learn to get			Increased self-esteem. I know that I am an interesting person and I don't have

	to know myself.		to depend on others for acceptance.
EXAMPLE 3 I hate . . . . (name of person).		forgive, accept and release this person from my angry thoughts.	Feeling of lightness and freedom as I release my anger and hatred. Increased self-respect.

2 Screaming Your Head Off

You haven't had time to change, accept or let go: you are *full of tension* and you are about to explode, probably inappropriately. We all know how this feels! Before you explode do the following exercise.

Go and find a quiet spot. Stretch your mouth as wide as you can and tense your facial, neck and head muscles. The rest of your body may also feel pretty tense too. Then, clench your fists and beat the air and *scream … silently!* Then totally relax and repeat. Do this until you feel better. You might even find yourself moved to laughter!

Let go of stress as quickly as you can, before it has time to affect you. Act quickly!

3 Moving On

When you are angry, upset, worried, tense … stop for a moment. Take a breather and ask yourself this question: 'Does it really matter?'

If it does then make sure you express your feelings to whoever needs to know. However, more often than not we allow ourselves to get worked up over the most trivial things, then we explode, then we feel even worse and so it goes on. Your child has dirt on his trousers; your partner has put the pans away in the wrong cupboard; the house isn't perfectly tidy ... Is it really worth making a point? Is it worth getting wound up?

The next time you become annoyed over a minor detail, take a breather and think again. Ask yourself, 'Does it really matter?' and if the answer is 'no' then say to yourself, 'This doesn't really matter', let go and move on.

4 Doing the 'You Can't Make Me' Swing

Children are naturally good at letting go of stress; they aren't afraid to make a scene or express their emotions. Whilst I'm not suggesting that you throw a tantrum in a shop, you could tap into your childish playfulness and rebelliousness with this little exercise which has a brilliant de-stressing and calming influence.

Stand with your feet apart (about the width of your shoulders). Swing your body, neck and head as one unit to the left and to the right. Let your arms swing freely as your body turns from side to side, so that they wrap round you at your shoulders. Make sure that your head follows your body as you swing. As your body swings from left to right and back, shout 'You can't make me!' as loud as possible. Really let go and enjoy yourself. Keep shouting. Try 'I don't care' or 'No I won't'.

This is a great way to release harmful emotions: it helps to stop us taking everything so seriously. Swing, shout and laugh and put things back into perspective.

5 Re-framing Your Situation

Remember that stress is not an outside influence but an inner feeling. If you can change the way you see your negative situations you can take the stress from your life.

14

STEP 1
Think of a personal situation which is a problem for you at the moment. It could be to do with work, family, a personal relationship ... choose something which is causing you worry and tension.

STEP 2
Find a quiet place, relax, close your eyes and visualize the problem in all its colourful glory. Now, take the person/situation/event and drain all the colour out of the picture.

STEP 3
Imagine the image getting smaller and smaller, shrinking until it has disappeared.

STEP 4
Now create a big, bold and colourful picture of you dealing brilliantly with the situation. See yourself looking confident, finding a resolution to the problem and feel your success.

Use this technique to reframe your negative pictures and take the stress out of your life.

• See the image.
• Drain the colour.
• Shrink the picture.
• See and feel a bright new positive image.

When stress is having a negative impact on your life act immediately to alter this situation. By identifying and understanding your stressors you can find constructive ways to eliminate their impact. If you are suffering from stress build-up at any time choose one of the stress-busting workouts that is appropriate for the occasion.

Take charge of your life, you don't *have* to suffer from stress.

KEY POWER POINTS

These key points are here to remind you of why you are doing your *De-stressing Your Life* workouts. Refer to this list for constant encouragement and support. Reclaim the power that is yours!

1 Stress is in the eye of the beholder. This is an empowering realization.
2 We all need a certain amount of stress (or challenge) in our lives. It encourages us to develop and grow and reach our potential.
3 Your stress has reached harmful levels when the quality of your life becomes affected. You know when this happens to you.
4 By identifying the unnecessary stressors in your life you can find ways to *let go*, *change*, or *accept* them. There is always a way to resolve your difficulties – you just need to recognize it.
5 Let go of stress as quickly as you can before it has time to affect you. Act quickly as soon as you feel the symptoms!
6 Whenever you are upset, tense or in conflict ask yourself, 'Does it really matter?' If not, let it go and move on. Life is too precious to waste in blame and recrimination.
7 Scream silently, swing ferociously, shout loudly and get in touch with your inner child; she knows how to get shot of stress!
8 Remember that stress is not an outside influence, it is an inner feeling. You can always change your feelings. You never need to become a stress victim!

3 Managing Your Time

Time waits for no woman.

- When you don't know whether you are coming or going.
- When your life feels muddled.
- When you are over-tired.
- For low self-esteem.
- For worry and stress.
- Whenever you feel out of control.
- When you are feeling dissatisfied with your life.

If you lead a busy life and don't organize your time, then sooner or later your busyness will overwhelm you. I know someone who created a serious sleep problem for herself because she didn't manage her time effectively. She had three children and worked full time and (in her words) 'just muddled along'. She started waking up at night in a panic and then she was unable to get back to sleep. She traced the panic attacks to a feeling that her life was running away with itself and she was 'out of control'. She spent many sleepless nights worrying about what she 'should' have done or 'must remember' to do. This is a common syndrome which easily develops as we increase our responsibilities, and which we have all experienced at some time or other.

The good news is that there is an easy solution to this problem – time management. But how well you manage your time will depend on how much you value it.

Remember, this is your own precious life. Time waits for

no woman so don't squander it. If your time is valuable then take control of how you use it. When you manage your time effectively you put a value on your time and effort, your self-esteem will increase and others will treat you with more respect.

HOW TO MANAGE YOUR TiME

Workout 1 will show you how to start taking control of your day. These techniques really help you to get a grip and feel much more organized. Workout 2 looks in detail at how you spend your time and whether you are doing the things you love to do. The last workout shows you how to stop procrastinating. This little habit can wreck your self-respect and cause all sorts of psychological and practical problems.

1 Organizing Your Life

1 Start to write things down. Buy a diary, calendar, pinboard. Write lists of things to do.

2 Look at the lists, pinboard, calendar and diary! (Most important.)

3 Prioritize your jobs. Number them in order of importance. Do you need to do everything on your list today? Do you *really* need to do all these things? If not, delete them.

4 Say 'no' to anything that you can't or don't want to do and say it immediately. Don't say a 'yes' that you don't mean and then spend time worrying about how you will (eventually) back out. This can definitely lead to sleepless nights! Women always need to practise saying 'no'. We are so keen to please others we often forget to please ourselves.

5 Take time out for yourself in the spaces in the day that

you have created by good time management. Value your time – don't just take on more work to fill the gaps.

2 Using Your Time Happily

Are you managing your time effectively and happily? Are you able to make time for the things you love to do? Try the following exercise

STEP 1

Look carefully at the way you use your precious time throughout your week. Make a time use pie chart by drawing a circle, about six inches in diameter, on a piece of paper. Think about how you use your time in different activities and divide up your 'pie'. The 'time use' diagram gives an example of how to do this.

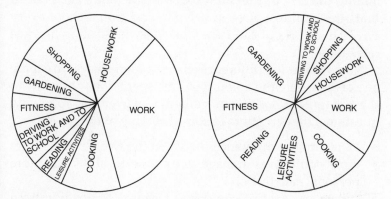

Figure 1. Time Use Pie Chart   *Figure 2. Fulfilment Gained Pie Chart*

STEP 2

Now put this chart aside. Using another piece of paper draw another circle and divide it up to represent those activities where you gain most fulfilment. This is your 'fulfilment gained' pie chart. Don't look at the first chart while you are drawing the second.

STEP 3
Put the charts side by side and see how they relate to each other. In the example we can see that there are some discrepancies between how much of the week is spent on some activities and the proportion of satisfaction gained. Work and housework take about half of the week's time but certainly don't provide 50 per cent of fulfilment. This lady would rather spend more of her time on gardening, keeping fit, reading and other leisure activities. This poses the question of where she can find the extra time. Perhaps she would rather job share than work full time? It might be possible to share some of the burden of the housework among the rest of the family. Could she join a car pool so that she wouldn't have to drive to and from school every day? This workout can raise some very interesting lifestyle questions.

Now look at the differences in your own charts. Are there any areas where the amount of time spent does not relate to the amount of fulfilment gained? Answer the following questions; they might take some thinking about.

- What are the differences between the two charts?
- How could you manage your time to allow for more personal satisfaction?
- When you do this could you face any opposition from other people in your life?
- How can you deal with these potential difficulties? Be prepared!

3 Just Doing It!
Procrastination creates low self-respect and takes up a lot of

your time. How many times a day do you think of that task that you keep putting off (letter that needs writing, phone call to make, desk that needs sorting ...?) If you had used the time you spent thinking about the things that you needed to do you could probably have done them all *and had time to put your feet up!*

One brilliant way to stop the procrastinating habit is to start to *just do it*. Before you can just do it you need to clear up all your unfinished jobs (half-read books, half-written poem, any creative inspirations which didn't quite make it ...). Sometimes it doesn't matter if you don't complete a project, perhaps it wasn't what you expected it to be. If that piece of knitting is a disaster just throw it away. We all have things that we think we 'should' finish and most of them are wind-ups. Give yourself a break: either throw them out and forget about them or finish them.

- Make a list of all your unfinished jobs.
- Decide which ones can hit the bin and then throw them away.
- Choose one of the rest and FINISH IT!
- When you have cleared the backlog you will feel amazingly virtuous and you will then be free to keep up to date with yourself.
- When the next job comes along *just do it*, and let just doing it become a habit. Your self-respect will reach dizzy heights.

If your life is in a chaotic muddle then you will feel that you never have enough time. This is the time of your life: live it and love it. Get organized. Manage the practicalities and you will have time to do the things you really want to do. You will have to keep lists and you may have to say 'no' more often than you are used to, but whose life is this anyway? Throw out all those half-finished, potentially brilliant creations that are lurking in polythene bags under the stairs. Let your motto become *'Just do it!'* Learn how to value your time and you will learn how to value yourself.

KEY POWER POINTS

These key points are here to remind you of why you are doing your *Managing Your Time* workouts. Refer to this list for constant encouragement and support. Reclaim the power that is yours!

1   If you don't organize your time you will run out of time.
2   This is the time of your life!
3   Time waits for no woman – don't squander it.
4   When you manage your time you put a value on yourself and others will treat you with more respect.
5   Say 'no' when you mean it. Time management relies on your ability to do this. Practise in front of the mirror if you need to. Women are natural pleasers and we have to train ourselves to be able to say no.
6   Prioritize your jobs and let go of the ones that don't really need to be done.
7   Enjoy the free time you create for yourself. Do the things you love to do.
8   Let your motto become *'just do it!'*
9   Love your life and value your moments, they are unrepeatable.

4 Becoming Confident

If you believe that you can do a thing, or if you believe that you cannot, in either case you are right.

Henry Ford

- When you can't trust yourself to make decisions.
- When you lose self-respect.
- When you compare yourself with others.
- Whenever you feel like a victim.
- When your relationships fall apart.
- Whenever you feel that you are not good enough.

You are what you believe you are, you will become what you expect to become – the choice is yours. On a good day, when everything falls into place, it's so easy to feel confident and high in self-belief; the world is your oyster. And then, quite suddenly sometimes, that precious magical feeling can just slip away. When we lose self-belief we look out onto a world where everyone else is getting their lives together: having brilliant relationships, being successful at work and having a great life whilst we are struggling in the depths of negativity. This isn't quite true of course because *everyone* suffers lack of self-belief sometimes. Some people react to this condition by becoming aggressive bullies and others (usually women) become submissive victims.

Women seem to struggle with issues of confidence far more than men. We seem to have a natural tendency to bring ourselves down rather than to lift ourselves up! Many of us have been taught that to be female is to be 'pretty/

wholesome/caring/supportive/nurturing/receptive ...'
etc. Our brothers are more likely to have been encouraged
to be outward-going, confident, goal-oriented and competitive. Times are changing and women's life expectations
mirror that change. You can increase your confidence by
changing your negative self-beliefs and by recognizing and
enhancing your unique strengths and gifts. You are a
unique and powerful woman – believe it!

HOW TO BECOME CONFIDENT

Workout 1 shows how you can change your negative self-
beliefs by making positive affirmations. Workout 2 reminds
you that you are a unique and special woman and Workout
3 asks you to list your strengths and successes.

1 Making a List of Positive Affirmations

Belief is strong magic.

When the going gets rough the tough make positive
affirmations! If we are low it feels impossible to believe that
we really are special, worthy and lovable. *But of course it is
always true!* It is at these times of difficulty that we most
need to believe in ourselves. Belief is very strong magic!
When you are feeling unworthy, not good enough (for
whom?), not clever enough, not beautiful enough, not
anything enough: when it feels impossible to love yourself,
then practise. Practise believing that you are amazing,
important, wonderful, creative, deserving, significant –
because you are. Create your own list of affirming self-
beliefs. Keep these affirmations in the present tense, keep
them positive and practise saying them all the time. Refer

to your list as soon as you feel your confidence slipping. Use the examples below if you wish and create some more of your own. Stick them up all over the house, keep reminding yourself.

AFFIRMATIONS:
I am good enough.
I am a wonderful woman.
I love and value myself.
I deserve the best in life.

My List of Positive Affirmations

1 ....

2 ....

3 ....

2 Remembering That You Are Unique

As soon as our confidence falls we start comparing ourselves with others. We go 'comparison shopping' where we 'buy into' the concept of a comparative scale of self-worth:

I'm not as talented as ... but I am more talented than ...
I'm not good enough/creative enough to do that ...

Do you ever do this? Every time you compare yourself with other people you are acting like a victim (and this can only end in tears!). How do you know if you are successful/ happy/clever/doing well/doing badly ... etc? No one else can be inside you. No one else can experience your self-satisfaction (or lack of it). Only you know what it feels like to be you. Stop comparison shopping, it will never increase your confidence. Whenever you start to compare yourself with someone else or with some mythical standard of perfection just become aware of what you are doing and *stop it!* Say instead, over and over again:

I am unique.

Enhance your originality. Whenever you feel the urge to try to 'fit in' in some way, look closely at whatever you feel makes you different. Accept and make the most of your differences. They are what make you a unique and original person with your own special place in the world.

3 Looking at the Good News About You

Let's let go of negative self-beliefs and focus on your strengths and successes. Never mind what you can't do, let's look at what you can do!

Complete the following:

- My best asset is my ...
- I feel sexy when ...
- The best thing about my personality is ...
- The thing I like best about my body is ...
- The most incredible thing I have ever done is ...
- I feel attractive when ...
- I feel powerful when ...

Reflect on your answers. When your confidence drops just remember your strengths and achievements; you have so much going for you.

When your self-belief disappears and your confidence falls remind yourself of your amazingness! Keep saying your positive affirmations, stop comparison shopping and remember that you are unique and utterly original. Focus on your strengths and you will find that there is always plenty of good news about yourself. Remind yourself of these things all the time (especially when you can't believe any of them) and it will eventually become easier and easier to pick yourself up, dust yourself down and start all over again.

KEY POWER POINTS

These key points are here to remind you of why you are doing your *Becoming Confident* workouts. Refer to this list for constant encouragement and support. Reclaim the power that is yours!

1 You are what you believe you are, you will become what you expect to become – the choice is yours.
2 Everyone has to cope with negative self-beliefs; some people hide their insecurity by acting as bullies, others act as victims.
3 Women seem to have a natural tendency to bring themselves down. We can change this inclination!
4 You can increase your confidence by changing your negative self-beliefs and by recognizing and enhancing your unique strengths and gifts.
5 You are a unique and powerful woman – just believe this! Belief is strong magic.
6 *You are good enough!* Make positive affirmations about yourself.
7 Stop comparison shopping. You are unique. Enhance your originality.

8 Look at your strengths and achievements. Reflect on your positive qualities. Remember that whatever you think about grows.

9 The more you practise these workouts the better your life will become. You will find it easier and easier to bounce back.

5 Enjoying the Good Things in Life

Two women looked out through their prison bars.
One saw mud
The other saw stars.

Prosperous (adj.): 1 flourishing; prospering. 2 rich; affluent;
wealthy. 3 favourable or promising.
                                    Collins English Dictionary

- If you are feeling insecure.
- If you have lost faith in people, the universe, yourself.
- When you are feeling unsupported.
- When life feels competitive.
- When you feel let down in any way.
- When you are facing your own limitations.
- When everything seems to be going wrong.

I love the word 'prosperous', it sounds so full of wellbeing
and confidence. Do you feel prosperous?

The feeling of prosperity does not depend on your wealth
but on how you see the universe. A person may be rich in
money but insecure about how to hang on to it, or wracked
by guilt and totally unable to enjoy their good fortune. On
the other hand, someone else who is poorer may know how
to enjoy what they have and so can make the very best of
their life. Which one is prospering? The rich are not always
leading fulfilled and happy lives.

Feel rich in the good things of life and they will be attracted to you.

You

Feel poor in your resources and that's the way you will stay.

Ask yourself this question: 'Is my universe overflowing and abundant or is it impoverished and marked by scarcity?'

It is true that people are starving and dying in wars. And yes, our planet abounds in toxic waste, the seas are being poisoned, the rainforests are being cut down and there are holes in the ozone layer. This is certainly the way things are, but why are they like this? There is a growing opinion that a mass belief in scarcity has created our planetary and personal problems. Humanity holds a mass belief that 'there will never be enough of everything to go round', and so we must fight for scarce resources and compete for our survival. We have created scarcity and limitation, they are only ideas. The universe is abundant: it has everything we need for us all to enjoy the good things in life.

We have created scarcity – let us create prosperity instead.

HOW TO ENJOY THE GOOD THINGS IN LIFE

Workout 1 checks your own beliefs about scarcity and abundance. Workout 2 shows you how to recognize the abundance of the universe and Workout 3 helps you to change any scarcity beliefs that are limiting you.

1 Checking Your Own World View
Put 'I believe that ...' before each statement and answer yes or no.

	Yes	No
• This is a world of plenty.		
• There will never be enough of everything to satisfy everybody.		

- The world is a safe place.
- People are starving, the world is running out of food.
- The universe supports me.

                                                    Yes   No

- Human nature is basically competitive and not co-operative.
- We have the power to transform the planet.
- Everyone looks after number one.
- I create my own reality.
- My life is a struggle, we are here to suffer.
- We all deserve the very best in life.
- Nothing I can do will change the world.

Is your world a scary place? Do you live in an abundant universe or are you bogged down in scarcity consciousness? Which way of looking at the world supports your self-esteem and makes you feel good? Which view of the world allows for the possibility of change and which one ensures that you will remain a victim who can never enjoy the good things in life? If your current world view is that of a victim, it need not remain that way. Having acknowledged it, you can begin to deal with it. You *can* change your beliefs!

2 Recognizing the Abundance of the Universe

AFFIRMATION: *The abundance of the universe is mine.*

Say this affirmation to yourself. Never mind if you don't believe it at first. Just let those negative thoughts go; they won't work for you.

Experience the abundance of the universe. There is just so much of everything. Open a tomato and see how many seeds are inside, so many plants from one fruit. Blow a

31

dandelion clock and watch the seeds fly. How many potential dandelions can you see? Our world is naturally prolific. There is no shortage of air unless we decide to pollute it. Everything in nature is in harmony and balance unless we decide to create imbalance. Always look for abundance and prosperity and the more you do this the more you will experience the good things in life. Just try it for a day and see what happens. If it works then try it again the next day.

3 Changing Your Scarcity Beliefs

If you can change your individual consciousness to one of prosperity instead of scarcity, you will attract empowering new energy into your life. Think prosperous and you will start to feel prosperous; feel prosperous and you will affect the energy of those around you. Beware of the words you use for they create your beliefs. Change your negative beliefs as they only create scarcity and limitation in your life.

When you are feeling impoverished in any way choose some of the following prosperity affirmations. Say them, sing them, think them, write them on pieces of coloured card and display them prominently ... fill your mind with prosperity. Expand your vision, embrace the benevolent energy of the universe and allow abundance to flow into your life.

AFFIRMATIONS OF PROSPERITY:
There are no limitations.
The more I give, the more I will receive.
Life is a celebration.
I deserve the best in life.
We can heal the planet.

There is always enough of everything to go round.
I can change my reality.
My high self-esteem enhances the lives of others.
We are here to learn and grow.
We are all connected.
Love and respect are infinite resources.
We are here to take care of each other.
My beliefs create the quality of my life.
Nature has abundant resources.
Self-transformation leads to global transformation.

Your awareness of abundance and prosperity conscious-ness can change your own life and also help to change the planet. We don't need to compete: we can co-operate. There is plenty of everything to go round. If our world governments abounded in abundance awareness just think how we could all prosper and flourish – we could all enjoy the good things in life, we could change the world. There are no limits!

KEY POWER POINTS

These key points are here to remind you of why you are doing your *Enjoying the Good Things in Life* workouts. Refer to this list for constant encouragement and support. Reclaim the power that is yours!

1 Always look for the stars!
2 Feel rich in the good things of life and they will be attracted to you.
3 We have created scarcity and limitation, these are only ideas. The universe is abundant.
4 The universe supports you: this is a world of plenty.

5   Go out and look for abundance: the more you look for it the more you will see!

6   Change your negative beliefs: they create a limited reality.

7   Think, say, sing, write your affirmations of prosperity: fill your mind with abundance. (Don't take my word that this works; just fill your mind with prosperous thoughts for a day and see what happens.)

8   We are all connected.

9   Self-transformation leads to global transformation.

10 We can change the world.

6 Developing Your Spirituality

You are reminded that you must first draw from the well to nourish and give to yourself. Then there will be more than enough to nourish others.

Ralph Blum

- Whenever you feel stress.
- When you feel powerless.
- When you can't seem to stop 'doing' things.
- For that feeling of 'there must be more to life than this'.
- When the 24-hour society just becomes too much for you to handle.
- When you crave peace and calm.
- When you are running so fast that you overtake yourself.
- When you can't get your act together.
- If you suffer with depression.
- When you just can't stop thinking about things.
- When it's hard to relax and let go.

We can try to satisfy our desires by 'doing' things out in the world. Most of us spend all of our waking moments working for, wishing for and enjoying what we feel are the good things in this life. The more material goods we have the more we want, but material goods will never satisfy our desires. The material world cannot answer all our needs because we also need nourishment of the spiritual kind. We develop our spirituality by getting in touch with our inner senses and so increasing our self-awareness.

You

What is easy for one person is difficult for another. Some people find it very easy to relate to the physical world; they are very good at 'doing'.

Others find it less easy to be action orientated – perhaps they are more in touch with their inner senses; these people may be good at 'being'.

We could say that our lives encompass the states of being and doing.

Doing describes activity *out* in the world.
Being describes awareness *within* the person.

To feel harmonious, happy and at one with our lives we need to balance our 'being' and 'doing'. Many of us are extreme 'doers' or extreme 'be-ers'. We are out of balance in some way and this will be reflected in our dissatisfaction with our lives. We can all balance our being and doing by developing our spiritual awareness.

HOW TO DEVELOP YOUR SPIRITUALITY

Answer the questions in Workout 1 and discover your own levels of doingness and beingness. The other workouts will focus on your inner awareness and look at ways to help you to become more balanced by developing your spirituality. Don't forget to enjoy this inner journey!

1 Checking Your Levels of Being and Doing
Answer yes or no to the following questions:

                                                    Yes   No
- I need to be on the go all the time.
- I often have sleeping problems.

- I am afraid to try new things.
- I suffer from stress.
- I am ultra-sensitive to others.
- I find worldly matters threatening.

                                                Yes   No

- I am shy.
- People think that I am aggressive.
- I have problems making relationships.
- I am self-conscious.
- I am a compulsive list maker.
- I often find myself withdrawing.
- I always like to stay in control.
- I have a lot of nervous energy.
- People think I am a passive person.
- I'm not good at dealing with money matters.

If you have answered yes to any of these statements then you have a tendency to the extreme in either your doing or your being. Which way do you go when you are under pressure? Do you try to hide from the world by withdrawing (an extreme be-er) or do you hide yourself in excessive activity (an extreme do-er)? We all fly to one extreme or another when we are under stress.

It's not wrong to behave in this way but it is interesting to recognize which 'way' you are inclined to go. Any behavioural extreme will undermine your power and your levels of confidence and self-belief will fall. Balance is the key and if you can adjust your doing and being you will create a balanced mixture of 'inner' and 'outer' activity.

2 Focusing on Your Inner Awareness

If your energy is out of balance you can easily correct this by working on your spiritual growth. When you are looking at your spiritual nature you are looking at your inner awareness. You need to ask yourself such questions as:

- What is the quality of my relationship with myself?
- How can I get to know my inner self?
- How can I be responsive to my inner needs?
- Am I prepared to spend time on myself?

As daughters, mothers, lovers, grandmothers, partners, workers, friends, we find ourselves in many different and demanding roles. Everyone seems to *need* us so much don't they? As chief nurturers and carers we women must learn to find some time for ourselves. Sometimes we set ourselves up to be so needed that we don't have time to look at our own needs and desires.

Look carefully at your life. Do you need to be needed? You can release some of the ties that bind you: you are not indispensable. You deserve to spend time responding to your own inner needs. If you do, you will return to your people responsibilities with renewed vigour and enthusiasm (which has got to be good news for everyone concerned).

3 Making a Positive Affirmation

AFFIRMATION: *I trust and respect myself and I deserve to satisfy my inner needs.*

The first step of your inner journey depends upon whether or not you think that you deserve to devote time exclusively to your own needs. You may encounter lots of personal resistance at first, with thoughts like:

- I don't have time.
- I don't know what I'd do.
- I'd feel too guilty to enjoy it.

Repeat the affirmation for as long as you need to. Write it, sing it, display it. Do whatever you find the most helpful. Say it enough times and soon you will believe that the time has come to look at and respond to your own needs. When this happens your inner journey has begun!

If you haven't got time for yourself who is going to have time for you?

4 Allocating 'Me' Time

'Me' time is spent on yourself alone. You may choose to spend it with other people but this time is not *for* others, it's just for you. If you find it difficult to find time for yourself then try, just for a week, to give yourself some time every day (even if it's just a few minutes to stand and stare). Keep a journal for the week and note the day, what you did, how long for and what it felt like.

Taking time for yourself is very important. If you want to develop your spiritual nature it is absolutely vital to allocate yourself some regular time to pursue this activity. As you find time to relax and to do things 'just for you' you will become increasingly aware of your own spirituality. As you develop spiritually you will balance your being and doing activities. This balance will increase your self-esteem and enhance your relationships. If you find it hard to take 'me' time just keep trying. Extend the time each day and before you know it you will be wondering how you ever managed to live without it!

5 Creating a Spiritual Experience

We can forge a direct link with the energy of the universe to experience a spiritual connection for ourselves. The intensity of this experience goes beyond feelings of relaxation: it takes us to a place deep within ourselves where we can meet our true spiritual nature. We can use a variety of techniques to make this connection. Disciplines such as yoga and t'ai chi, which still the mind, can open our spiritual eyes. Meditation techniques can put us in touch with the universal energy, but sometimes people find meditation a daunting prospect. If you find it difficult to connect with your spirituality, try this simple but effective approach.

STAGE 1

Sit comfortably in a relaxed state and close your eyes. Watch your mind at work; just let it wander. Observe your thoughts and then let them go. Those thoughts will just keep on coming, so don't try to stop them. If your attention gets hooked by a thought you will eventually realize this and then you can let go of it (it's quite amazing to watch the constant working of our mind).

There are no right and wrong ways to approach your spiritual growth. Spiritual experiences will come when you are ready for them; the most important factor is your intention to develop. Self-criticism about the quality of your experience or the length of time you meditate will block your development. Be easy on yourself: the more you love yourself and the less you criticize yourself the greater your spiritual growth. Any time which you can spend alone in silence, observing your thoughts, feelings and emotions is time well spent. Slowly but surely your spiritual nature will blossom and you will be amazed at your inner world.

Try Stage 1 for ten minutes a day for a week and see how you go. When you are comfortable with this you might like to move on to stage 2 for ten minutes a day. If you wish to sit for longer periods then do so.

STAGE 2

Stage 2 develops the inner process further. Sit as before and let your mind wander. Concentrate on the rhythm of your breathing. Follow your in-breath and then your out-breath. Become aware of your breathing. As you breathe in think 'in' and as you breathe out think 'out'. In, out, in, out. Each time your mind wanders off, follow it, observe that it has wandered and then come back to your breathing. In, out, in, out.

Become aware of the place *between* the breaths – when you are not breathing in and not breathing out. Now concentrate on this place. Keep watching your breath but move your awareness to this place between the in- and out-breath. When your mind wanders off, follow it and then come back to your in- and out-breaths. Follow the in-breath and then the out-breath until you have regained a comfortable rhythm. Now return your concentration to the place between the breaths.

Practise these two stages. Become comfortable with Stage 1 before you move on to Stage 2. Encourage yourself at all times, especially if you are having difficulties. Remember that the most important issue in your self-development is *always* the strength of your intention. If you really want to develop your spirituality then you will; all the information you need will appear as you need it! It really is a magical process. This 2-stage action plan will work for you when you are ready for it and you will know when you are ready because you will enjoy the process.

There is so much more to life than what you see. The 'things' of this world will never completely satisfy you because you have a spiritual hunger. Look inside yourself and tap into your inner awareness. The techniques for this are very easy, you just need to find a few minutes a day for yourself to practise. Remember, if *you* can't find the time to address your inner needs then neither will anyone else. Whatever you value in yourself will be valued by others. Develop your spirituality and your ordinary life will become extraordinary!

KEY POWER POINTS

These key points are here to remind you of why you are doing your *Developing Your Spirituality* workouts. Refer to this list for constant encouragement and support. Reclaim the power that is yours!

1 Material goods will never satisfy your desires: the more you get the more you will want.
2 If you are always rushing about 'doing' things you need to find some time to stand and stare and just 'be'. Remember we are called human beings and not human doings.
3 If you constantly withdraw your energy whenever you face a challenge, then you also need to balance your 'being' and 'doing'. Developing your spirituality will make you feel more solid and grounded and able to act.
4 Your spirit needs attention and nourishment. If you neglect your spirit you will always feel disappointed and unfulfilled.
5 It is easy to get in touch with your spiritual nature, you just need a few minutes to yourself every day.

6 Be prepared to give yourself the time you need to develop your inner awareness. You deserve to satisfy your inner needs. Keep repeating the affirmation in the workouts.

7 If you still find it hard to take personal time, just check on your need to be constantly needed. Do people really need your time *all* of the time?

8 Keep a journal for a week and note your experiences during your 'me' time. It won't be long before taking personal time will become second nature to you and you won't know how you ever survived without it.

9 Taking space for yourself is also very good training for all your dependants. As you become spiritually stronger they become more independent.

Your Relationships

7 Checking Your Relationships – Are They Healthy?

And stand together yet not too near together:
for the pillars of the temple stand apart,
And the oak tree and the cypress grow not in
each other's shadow.

Kahlil Gibran

- When you find yourself in an unhappy relationship.
- When you are low in self-esteem.
- When you feel like a victim in any area of your life.
- If you find it hard to know when to stand up for yourself.
- When it's difficult for you to make decisions.

A healthy relationship is one that allows you to satisfy your basic needs: it lets you feel free to be yourself. What are your needs in a relationship? What do you like? What can't you bear? How far do you want to go with someone else? You will have different boundary lines with different people. Perhaps you don't disclose much about your private life to your work colleagues. You might find it easy to tell your best friend everything, or maybe you hold some things back. You may have experienced a feeling of being swamped by someone in an intimate relationship: you know, when you can't decide if *you* really want to do something or if you are only agreeing because your partner wants to do it.

It is always a good idea to keep a check on the way relationships are going (this includes all relationships:

family, lovers, friends, work colleagues). Are your needs being met? Sometimes it's difficult to recognize your needs and one way to make this easier is to become aware of our own personal boundaries. A boundary or limit is the distance you can comfortably go in a relationship (it can be physical, emotional, mental or spiritual, or a combination of any of these).

Once you become aware of your boundaries you can start to get to know who you are and what you want. Until you know who you are and what you want it will be impossible for you to know what is right and what is wrong for you in any relationship. You will be unable to have a healthy relationship of any sort (casual, close or intimate) because you won't know where you end and the other person begins. Look at the diagram opposite which shows the difference between healthy and unhealthy boundaries.

Figure 3 represents a meeting between you and me. Diagram (a) shows you and me just as we are first appearing in each other's lives. Our separate boundaries represent the whole of ourselves (mind, body, spirit and emotions). Space lies between us. Diagram (b) shows us coming together and interacting. We are sharing some space but our boundaries are intact and we are having a healthy relationship. Diagram (c) shows an invasion of our boundaries: our personal limits have been blurred. My boundaries and yours have become intermixed. The relationship is unhealthy because neither of us has a true sense of self any more. Where do you end and I begin? Do I want this or are we doing it because you want to? Look at Workout 1 and answer the questionnaire to see just how healthy your own boundaries are.

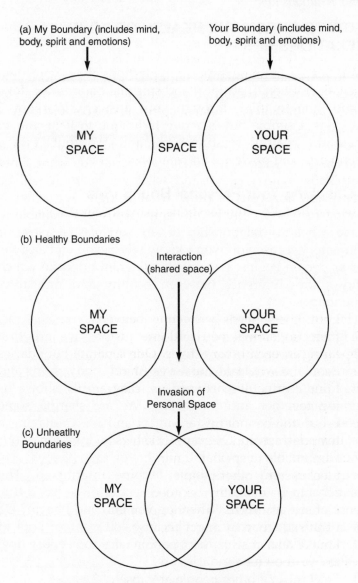

Figure 3. Healthy and Unhealthy Boundaries

HOW TO CHECK THE HEALTH OF YOUR RELATIONSHIPS

Workout 1 asks some important questions about your own mental, emotional, physical and spiritual boundaries. Take some time to think through your answers. Workout 2 suggests a simple but effective technique to help you to maintain healthy relationships, and Workout 3 is a wonderful and powerful affirmation.

1 Checking Your Personal Boundaries

Answer the following questions, using these options:

- Untrue
- Sometimes true
- Often true
- True

1	I put others' needs before my own.	_____
2	I am good at making decisions.	_____
3	I feel responsible for other people.	_____
4	People seem to take me for granted.	_____
5	I find it difficult to express my true feelings.	_____
6	I seem to put a lot into my relationships and get very little back.	_____
7	I am unable to speak my mind.	_____
8	I feel used by other people.	_____
9	I like to make others feel good.	_____
10	I am not victimized by other people.	_____
11	I am frightened by angry feelings.	_____
12	I make relationships with people who are no good for me.	_____
13	I feel upset if other people are upset.	_____

14 I am afraid to spend time alone. _____

15 Criticism really hurts me. _____

16 I do not stay in abusive relationships. _____

17 I don't trust myself. _____

18 I am very sensitive to the moods of
    others. _____

19 I find it difficult to keep a secret. _____

20 I can enjoy the successes of others. _____

Think carefully about how each of your answers affects the quality of your relationships. Look in particular at the behaviour and feelings which you think create a problem in your interactions with others: these are the areas where your boundaries are weak. Wherever you have a boundary problem you will also have low self-esteem. Poor relationships, unhealthy boundaries and low self-esteem go hand in hand. If you are in an unsatisfactory relationship and you are blaming the other person, you are a victim. Stop being a victim by changing your focus.

Look at your own behaviour, check your boundaries, take responsibility for your own needs and the quality of your relationships will change dramatically. As you become self-aware your self-esteem will rise. Increase your self-esteem and you will attract healthy relationships. If you respect yourself others will respect you.

2 Drawing Your Line in the Sand

Sometimes it can be very hard to decide whether your needs come before or after the needs of someone else. Every situation is different, but there is a process that you can use to help you to decide exactly how far you will go for another person, or in other words where you will draw your own line in the sand.

Imagine that a friend has asked for your help. They need you to do something for them but you have already planned a trip which you have been looking forward to. What can you do in a situation like this? If you abandon your own plans so that you can help, are you being a good friend or are you just being a victim who can't say 'no'?

Check that you are acting from the best possible motives and not because you are allowing yourself to be victimized. Carefully examine the situation and your feelings. If you are saying 'yes' but you experience fear, intimidation, anger, irritation, resentment, helplessness or low self-esteem, then it's time for you to draw a new line in the sand. Create a new boundary line with this person – I will go this far and no further. A good friend will respect your decision and a friend who doesn't is no real friend at all.

You will never be able to form good, healthy relationships if you are always trying to please other people instead of yourself.

3 Making a Positive Affirmation

You are a wonderful, caring and loving person who deserves to have supportive and nurturing relationships. Do you believe this to be true? Perhaps, deep down, you don't feel that you deserve love and support. Well, you do! We all do. If this is hard to believe then change this negative thought.

Write the following affirmation over and over again. Look into a mirror and say it to yourself. Sing it in the shower, in the car, on the bus (under your breath). Keep at it, it really works!

AFFIRMATION: *I . . . . (your name) am a wonderful, caring and loving person and I deserve to have supportive and nurturing relationships.*

Don't let yourself be taken for granted. Whenever you hit a relationship problem just stop and check your own personal boundaries. Have your priorities shifted? Do you need to draw a new line in the sand? Forget about being a people pleaser, you will only feel victimized and become resentful. Always respect your own needs and you will find that others will respect them too. Repeat the affirmation whenever you can and eventually it will become true for you.

KEY POWER POINTS

These key points are here to remind you of why you are doing your *Checking Your Relationships* workouts. Refer to this list for constant encouragement and support. Reclaim the power that is yours!

1 When you are in a healthy relationship you feel free to be yourself. Let this be a marker for you to measure the quality of each of your relationships. Ask yourself, 'Am I free to be me when I am with this person?' If the answer is 'no' then it's time to check your boundaries.

2 Whenever you have a boundary problem you will also have low self-esteem. Work on your self-awareness and your self-esteem will rise.

3 Increase your self-esteem and you will attract good, supportive relationships. When you respect yourself others will respect you.

4 Stop blaming others for your problems. A blamer is a victim. Change your focus and check your own behaviour.

5 Empower yourself by taking responsibility for your own needs: the nature of your relationships will change dramatically.

6 People pleasers never have good relationships. Always check your motives before you act. Are you doing something because you really want to, or are you being victimized?

7 Don't be afraid to stand up for yourself. This is your own precious life, don't waste it!

8 *I am a wonderful, caring and loving person who deserves to have supportive and nurturing relationships.* Make this affirmation all the time, even if you don't believe it (especially if you don't believe it!). Eventually this positive belief will replace the negative thoughts you have about yourself.

8 Changing Yourself

It's never too late to be what you want to be!

- Whenever you are feeling stuck somewhere in your life.
- When you feel that you are losing control.
- If your life feels flat and boring: if *you* feel flat and boring!
- Whenever you fear change.
- For low self-esteem.
- When you feel like re-inventing yourself.
- When nothing in your wardrobe looks right.
- If you haven't changed your hairstyle for more than a year.
- Whenever you feel that you are too old to do something.

There is a common syndrome that women share which I call *being stuck in treacle boots*. Imagine yourself wearing huge, leaded boots and standing in a great puddle of heavy, gluey treacle: it is virtually impossible to move. So many women have described to me this feeling of virtual immobility.

You wake up in the morning and *nothing* feels possible except inertia: you can't make any decisions, you lack clarity, you can't get a grip on anything ... I know that you know this feeling! Why do you feel like this? What can you do about it?

Whenever you find yourself stuck in treacle boots it's time to *change something in your life*. This syndrome comes upon us when our habitual daily patterns grind us into the ground and it all becomes too mundane. When we feel like this we need to shift some energy to get going again.

Everything changes and so do we, and if we don't move with this energy we feel left behind, stuck, ordinary, bored, miserable, ineffective ... It is easy to get out of treacle boots, you just need to introduce change into your life. Small changes will start the process. Self-change, even in small ways, starts a new process which can pull you out of negativity as new possibilities emerge on your horizon. You *can* change your life.

HOW TO CHANGE YOURSELF

Our daily habits help us to keep things together but sometimes they can stop us from having new experiences and expanding our lives. Workout 1 looks at how you can recognize and change minor habits and so start a new energetic process. Workout 2 shows you how to go about re-inventing yourself and Workout 3 looks at the limiting effect of a negative self-concept and how this can easily be changed.

1 Breaking a Habit

The smallest steps we take can have the greatest impact upon our lives. When you are feeling stuck just decide to change something, *anything* about your life. Choose something which seems to be small and insignificant. Break a minor habit. Don't try to do anything drastic like ending a relationship or stopping smoking. You are looking for a small change here, one that will not cost much energy but will introduce a new process of change. Here are a few suggestions:

• Cook a meal that is new to you. Enjoy investigating new ingredients.

- Go to work by a different route.
- Put the toilet roll on the holder the opposite way. Were you even aware that you always put it on the same way?
- Change sides in bed. This small change can feel enormous!
- Buy a different loaf of bread.

Find your own changes. Don't do anything that makes you feel too insecure. The important thing is that you start to become aware of your habits.

2 Re-inventing Yourself

One of the great things about going on holiday is that because no one knows you, you can be free to be different.

We can so easily become reflections of what other people expect of us and this can lead to us staying stuck in the same old groove. For example, if your image is neat, quiet and respectable, it's difficult suddenly to decide to go a bit wild. Our friends and loved ones get alarmed when we behave out of character and so, if it gets too uncomfortable to make a change, we just slip back into our usual image.

However, you don't have to go on holiday or move away from loved ones to be free to be different. Stop doing what you do just because you always do it like that! Give your life a buzz. Dare to be different. Do something which is out of character. Here are a few ideas.

- Change your dress style. If you always wear jeans try something more formal. If you always wear smart clothes, relax your dress code.
- Make a new friend and choose someone who is not at all like you.
- Start a new hobby or join a nightclass.
- Change your hairstyle. This can be a scary but very

effective technique! It really makes you feel like a different person.

- Do you always wear dark colours? Wear something bright and feel the difference.
- Go to a different pub/restaurant.
- Change your makeup, or better still don't wear any! This will feel *really* different. Try it just once and experience the different way you feel.

Start with small changes and you will be amazed by how these will affect you. If being different is difficult at first, just keep practising. Change is like a breath of fresh air. Climb out of those treacle boots and enjoy your new perspectives.

3 Changing Your Negative Self-Image

How do you see yourself? Do you feel successful, energetic, decisive, intelligent, thoughtful, creative and in charge of your life? You are all of these things and more! Only your limiting self-beliefs stand in your way. Think of three things that you feel you are no good at. There, now wasn't that easy! You could probably think of a hundred and three. Now think of three things that you are really good at. Ah, not quite so easy. There is no doubt that women in general find it very hard to be upbeat about themselves. Consciously start to think and say positive instead of negative things about yourself. Replace your negatives with positives.

EXAMPLES
Replace
I'm no good at ...   with *I am getting better at...*
I always make a mess of things with *I always learn from my mistakes*
I can't   with *I'll do the best I can*

| *I always lose out* | with *I am a winner* |
| *My life is so boring* | with *I can change my life* |

Change the way that you think and talk about yourself and your life will change. Many of the negative beliefs you hold about yourself are only things that you have *learned* to believe as you were growing up. If a belief doesn't work for you then let it go. Beliefs are only thoughts and thoughts can be changed. Go for a positive self-image and notice that people treat you with greater respect. Don't give up on this workout: keep practising, for life!

Your life is an amazing experience: everything changes and so do you. If you are feeling stuck then it's time to change something in your life. Small changes lead to enormous changes, so start breaking some minor habits. Become a new you: re-invent yourself. Forget about what other people might think and discover some new dimensions within yourself. Change your negative self-beliefs or they will keep you stuck!

KEY POWER POINTS

These key points are here to remind you of why you are doing your *Changing Yourself* workouts. Refer to this list for constant encouragement and support. Reclaim the power that is yours!

1　When you feel stuck it's time to change something in your life.
2　When your habitual daily patterns grind you into the ground you just need to shift some energy in order to get yourself going again.

3 Everything changes and so do you: you always need to move with this energy.
4 Small changes start a new process as different possibilities emerge on your horizon.
5 You *can* change your life.
6 Break a habit and see where this leads you.
7 Re-invent yourself. Dare to be different and climb out of those treacle boots.
8 Change is like a breath of fresh air. Enjoy the new perspectives that it brings.
9 Only your limiting self-beliefs stand in your way. Change them and change your life forever!

9 Changing Your Personal Relationships

But relationships are not outside – they are inside of us; this is the simple truth that we must recognize and accept. My true relationship is with myself – all others are simply mirrors of it.

Shakti Gawain

- When you feel that you need to change your life.
- For difficulties in your personal / work / family relationships.
- When you want someone to change.
- When you think you know exactly *how* someone should change.
- Whenever you are feeling disempowered.

If only I could find the right man/woman I would be so happy. If only my parents would change then everything would be OK. If only my boss was less stressed out, then work would be great. If only the children would be more respectful ... Oh if only I could change everyone then I would be so happy!

Who or what would you like to change in order to make your relationships work? Fill in the following table.

The Ways I Would Like People To Change

Name	I would like this person to be:
. . . .	. . . .
. . . .	. . . .
. . . .	. . . .
. . . .	. . . .

How can you change these people? The truth is that you can't change them and the more you try the worse it gets. Whenever you are waiting for someone to change you will be low in self-esteem. If your happiness depends upon the action of others you have become a victim, you are disempowered, you have lost direction and self-respect. We become trapped when we look for fulfilment anywhere *outside* ourselves.

It *is* possible to change your relationships but you need to take a totally different approach.

HOW TO CHANGE YOUR PERSONAL RELATIONSHIPS

The following workouts will focus on the part you play in creating your relationships. Workouts 1 and 2 look at your past behaviour and Workout 3 shows you a new approach which will help you to create new, improved personal relationships.

1 Changing Another Person

Think of a time when you tried to change another person.

1   The behaviour I wanted to change was:

. . . .

. . . .

2   I tried to change this behaviour by:

. . . .

. . . .

3   The outcome of this situation was:

. . . .

. . . .

Can you describe the type of relationship you now have with this person?

4   Our relationship now is:

. . . .

. . . .

Did your attempts to change this person have any effect on your relationship? If so, what happened?

5   Our relationship changed in the following ways:

. . . .

. . . .

It is only possible to make changes in a relationship if you yourself are prepared to change the messages that you are sending to the other person. If you are being victimized in a personal relationship then you have allowed this to happen: at some level you have shown the other person that this is what you think you deserve. If you are focusing on the behaviour of the other person you are looking in the wrong direction!

2 Choosing to Stay in a Poor Relationship
Have you ever stayed in an unhappy relationship? If so, can you describe it?

1   This relationship is/was unsatisfactory because:

. . . .

. . . .

2　I tried to change this relationship.　　　　Yes/No

3　I chose to stay in this relationship because:

. . . .

. . . .

4　My feelings about the other person in the relationship are:

. . . .

. . . .

5　I am still in this relationship.　　　　　Yes/No

6　My feelings about myself are:

. . . .

. . . .

7　I would describe myself as a powerful/disempowered woman.

3　Changing Your Focus

The ways people treat us are reflections of the ways that we treat ourselves.

This is a wonderful liberating truth that can free you from the shackles of any relationship. Change your focus from the *outside* to the *inside*. Relationships are not made outside but inside ourselves. The only true relationship is the one which you have with yourself: all of your relationships are a reflection of this one.

Look at your relationships. In what ways do you feel mistreated?

. . . .

. . . .

Now, think about the ways that you treat yourself. If, for example, you feel that you are not treated with respect, look inside and ask yourself if you have self-respect. If you treat yourself badly then others will do the same. If you victimize yourself you will be sure to attract the sort of people who are looking for a victim.

Look again at your relationships. In what ways do you feel supported?

. . . .

. . . .

Now, think about the ways that you support yourself. If you truly appreciate your strengths then others will reflect that appreciation. In other words, treat yourself well and others will do the same: victimizers will leave your life (if you haven't left them first).

When a relationship becomes difficult always ask yourself this question: 'How have I attracted this behaviour into my life?'

When you stop trying to blame others for your poor relationships and turn the focus of your attention on yourself there may be an initial sense of loss – a loss of potential excitement/danger/the unknown. We are so attracted to giving our power away (particularly to men!). The pattern of our present relationships is closely linked with the relationships we had with our parents. As tiny baby girls we were very sensitive to the emotional vibrations of our parents. As soon as we became aware of our parents' emotional pain we did all we could to make it right for them. We tried to keep them happy so that they would carry on looking after us. This felt like a survival issue to the tiny, vulnerable and needy baby girl and so pleasing our parents became vitally important.

Until we become consciously aware of this issue, *all* our future intimate relationships will have this underlying theme. It goes like this: 'I will try to be what you want me to be if you will stay with me and give me what I need.'

Do you recognize this theme in any of your relationships? If you do, then you must know by now that this way of running relationships never works. People can't always be what we want them to be and so we feel let down. We may then try to change them or we may give up, submit and become resentful, or we may leave and look for someone else who we think will give us what we need.

If you have tried unsuccessfully to change the nature of a relationship and you still find yourself emotionally involved, then investigate your motives. Are you living out the underlying theme which you developed with your parents when you were a baby? Do you need to please people? Do you need to be 'looked after'?

Stop looking for Prince Charming, he doesn't exist! Only you can give yourself the care and nurturing which you really need. You are no longer a baby. Take responsibility for yourself – don't give your power away. Change the focus of your energy and know that you attract the relationships that you deserve.

KEY POWER POINTS

These key points are here to remind you of why you are doing your *Changing Your Personal Relationships* workouts.

Refer to this list for constant encouragement and support. Reclaim the power that is yours!

1 Your most important relationship is the one that you have with yourself – all the rest are simply mirrors of it.

2 You cannot change anybody! People can only change themselves and they will only do that when *they* want to.

3 If you are waiting for someone to change you are giving your power away. Stop waiting, start changing or leave the relationship. You can't? Oh yes you can!

4 It *is* possible to change your relationships: look to change yourself.

5 People treat us the way we teach them to treat us. Teach them well.

6 If you victimize yourself you will attract victimizers (who will be magnetically attracted to you). Give up your victim status and potential victimizers will keep out of your life. This works like magic.

7 When a relationship becomes difficult always ask yourself this question: 'How have I attracted this behaviour into my life?' Change yourself to change your relationships.

8 You don't need to please people so that they will 'look after' you: you are not a baby girl any longer. Claim your woman power and become your own best friend.

9 Prince Charming doesn't exist and all the time you spend looking for him you are giving your power away!

10 Balancing Your Male and Female Energy

I contradict myself. I am large. I contain multitudes.

Walt Whitman

- When you are feeling over-sensitive and vulnerable.
- When you are feeling low in confidence.
- If you think that you are either the dominant or submissive partner in your intimate relationships.
- When you have lots of creative ideas but can't seem to put them into action.
- If you think that you are too pushy or too passive in any area of your life.

Are you attracted to action-orientated and dominating males or do you like men who need mothering? Do you usually express your feelings or are you inclined to keep them to yourself? Are you very intuitive and, if so, does this ability sometimes make it hard for you to act?

We can only enjoy balanced relationships and be confident to express our feelings and ideas when our own energies are balanced. Ancient Eastern philosophies and modern Western psychology have taught that we each have female and male energies within us. Both women and men are a combination of female and male energy. Our female energy is inner-directed, spiritual and emotional, wise and instinctive, and we become aware of it through our intuition. Our male energy is more outward-looking and active, and combines logic, rationality and practicality.

In the past our traditionally male-dominated society has only valued the masculine energies of logic, thought, rationality and action. Our all-important feminine energies of spiritual and emotional awareness have been ignored and even denied. Happily times are changing and the importance of personal, spiritual and emotional balance is now being recognized by men as well as women!

Women and men are psychologically balanced when they embrace both the female and male sides of their natures. When a woman is balanced she is emotionally and spiritually aware *and also* strong, decisive and active. There are many women today who have taken powerful roles within society by combining their inner wisdom (female side) with strength and assertiveness (male side).

The majority of women relate heavily to their female side and lack male energy and the majority of men relate largely to their male side and lack female energy. Most women need to become more assertive and risk-taking (male energy) and most men need to get in touch with their feelings (female energy).

HOW TO BALANCE YOUR MALE AND FEMALE ENERGIES

These workouts will help you to develop both your male and female energies. The first two techniques will help you to develop your male energy and the next two will help you to use your female energy in the most productive way. (Sometimes our female energy is so powerful it can get out of control.)

1 Writing Your Action Plan
If you don't have a destination you can never arrive! Where

are you going in your life? What would you really like to do? Whatever your goals you can bring them closer by writing an action plan. When we commit ourselves on paper we take ourselves much more seriously.

Divide a piece of paper into five columns with the following headings:

INTENTION METHOD NEEDS   REVIEW CHANGES

Intention: State your target. I want to ....

Method: Decide what steps you need to take. List them in order.

Needs: List all the resources you may need, eg help, advice, finance, family support ... Your list may change as time passes

Review: Give yourself some realistic deadlines. Decide on certain dates to check your progress.

Changes: Note any changes that become needed as you go on. This is your flexibility column and will affect the rest of your plan. Be prepared to adapt your plan so that you can respond creatively to change instead of being floored by the first hiccup.

Choose a relatively short-term goal and as you activate your plan you will become increasingly confident in your ability to 'make things happen'. Step by step you can put your ideas into practice instead of just thinking about them. Become an action-taker and feel your energy and your life change.

2 Saying 'No'

'No' is such a small word, but it seems to be one of the hardest words for us to say. Do you ever say 'yes' when you really want to say 'no'? If you don't say what you mean you will become a passive (and angry) victim. Women have such a struggle to balance their energy in this area: it's a question of equating our caring and nurturing instincts with the ability to make sure our own needs are met. Stick with it, I can promise you that saying 'no' becomes easier and easier the more you practise.

1 *Practise saying 'no'*: say it out loud to yourself when there's no one around, just get used to saying it.
2 *Imagine a situation where you want to say 'no'*: see the person in your mind's eye and visualize yourself saying 'no' to them.
3 *Say it for real*: the first time you say your 'no' for real it might feel a bit scary. As soon as you say it congratulate yourself, don't apologize! Don't back down. You will feel fantastic. Remember, you can be a good friend and still say 'no'.

3 Stepping into a Bubble of Light

Sometimes when our female energies are not centred we can feel exposed and unprotected and very sensitive to others. When you are feeling vulnerable try this great technique.

Close your eyes and slow your breathing. Now imagine yourself standing in front of an open window. You see a bubble come floating through this window. Notice the colour of your bubble. It floats to the floor in front of you and, as you watch, it grows in size and beauty until it is bigger than you. Now step into your bubble. You are feeling totally protected. You know that nothing and no one can harm you when you are inside your beautiful bubble.

You can do this visualization at any time, anywhere. After you have done it a few times it will only take a few seconds to 'see' your bubble and 'feel' it protectively surrounding you.

4 Relaxing

You might find at times that your male energy overrides your female energy. If you feel that you are sometimes over pushy or dominating, you may have overcompensated and become aggressive instead of assertive. This can easily happen when you need to make your mark in a male-dominated situation. Being over-forceful only leads to headaches and confrontation. Learn a relaxation technique such as meditation, yoga, t'ai chi, visualization or breathing exercises. Go to a class or choose some of the relaxation techniques from this book. Feel the beneficial effects of your female energy and balance yourself. You *can* be effective and powerful as long as you remember to keep in touch with your spiritual and emotional energy.

Whenever you are afraid to take a risk recognize that you need to call on your own male energy. Remember that you have these dynamic qualities and that you can make things happen. If you are becoming overpowering and your female energy is flagging, just turn your attention inwards and call upon your intuitive feminine side. When your female energy gets out of control and you feel vulnerable and exposed, protect yourself by stepping into a bubble of light. Learn to balance yourself and your life will take on new meaning.

KEY POWER POINTS

These key points are here to remind you of why you are doing your *Balancing Your Male and Female Energy* workouts. Refer to this list for constant encouragement and support. Reclaim the power that is yours!

1 You can only enjoy balanced relationships if your own energy is balanced.

2 If you are lacking in confidence and find it hard to make your mark in the world then you are lacking male energy. Most women have this problem. Let this hearten you.

3 Your highly developed spiritual and emotional intelligence is your most powerful tool, as long as you also integrate your male energies.

4 You can learn to develop male energy. Start to write personal action plans, they help to transform creative impulses into reality.

5 Practise saying 'no'. This little word will become a stepping stone into an assertive lifestyle. Don't miss out this workout!

6 You can still be a good friend and say 'no'. Balance your desire to care for others with your own personal needs.

7 Whenever you are being passive you are being a victim (and you are feeling angry).

8 When your female energy gets out of control and you feel vulnerable, exposed and over-sensitive, consciously work on your spiritual side.

9 Empowered women combine their inner wisdom (female side) with strength and assertiveness (male side). Look out for the men who are doing this too, they make wonderful partners!

10 Scientific research shows that women can automatically direct emotions to a part of the brain that can allow them to talk about their feelings. *Men can't do this*, which is no surprise to most of us! So have patience, men also have to work at learning to balance their energies.

11 Trusting Yourself and Others

The real voyage of discovery consists not in seeking new landscapes but in having new eyes.

Marcel Proust

- When your self-belief and self-respect are low.
- When you are feeling unsafe.
- When you feel unworthy and 'just not good enough'.
- If you are not using your incredible intuitive gifts.
- If you are facing changes and/or setbacks in your life.
- When the fear of failure stops you from acting.

Self-belief is the key ingredient of a successful and happy life. When we have it we feel on top of the world: calm, confident and in control and the world is our oyster. We feel good about ourselves, we feel we deserve the best and we attract good fortune into our lives (people like a winner). When we lose our self-belief we lose all these marvellous feelings and everything starts to go wrong. We all know only too well how this feels. So how can we hang on to our self-belief and keep a positive outlook?

We value ourselves only as highly as we can trust ourselves and our world. Self-trust maintains our self-belief. Do you trust yourself? Sometimes our personal trust levels alter in different areas of our lives. For example, you may trust yourself in the workplace but find it harder to do so in your personal relationships. You might have experienced a setback which has knocked your self-trust to pieces: illness, bereavement, separation and any major change in your lifestyle can do this.

When you look at a newborn baby you know that a miracle has happened. Look at the unconditional trust in that baby's eyes; what self-belief! You were once that newborn child. What has happened to take away your intrinsic worthiness? Nothing external has happened: the only change lies in your own perceptions.

HOW TO START TRUSTING YOURSELF AND OTHERS

Workout 1 is in two parts. The first part looks at your present levels of trust: your answers will reflect some of the deep beliefs you have held since childhood. The second part will then take you a step further and ask *why* you believe these things to be true. Workouts 2, 3 and 4 are all about learning to listen to, trust and act upon that powerful female instinct, your intuition.

1 Checking Your Levels of Trust

PART A

Look at the checklist below and answer yes or no to each question. On a good day your answers might be different to those you give when you are feeling not so good. Try to tap into your most powerful beliefs, the ones that run you most of the time.

                                     Yes   No

- I believe in myself.
- I usually know the right thing to do.
- I trust my intuition.
- I always do the best I can.

- I learn from my mistakes.
- I am safe.
- The universe supports me.

Do you believe these things to be true for you? Most of our ways of thinking about ourselves and our world have been learned by us whilst we were very little girls. If your first few years were spent in a supportive environment and you were well nourished (physically, mentally, emotionally and spiritually) then it is likely that you will be able to contact a feeling of safety deep within you in your adulthood. If for any reason your early childhood was lacking in love and care and positive approval you will probably be low in self-belief and find it hard to say and believe that, 'I am safe' or that 'the universe supports me'.

PART B
Go back through the checklist and think carefully about the way you answered.

- Why did you reply the way that you did?
- What is difficult for you to believe and why?
- What is easy for you to believe and why?

Positive self-belief requires that you trust yourself and your world. Trust is a big word; it involves a commitment to holding positive beliefs about the universe at a very deep level; it requires an intimate relationship with your inner self. One way to help you to develop your inner stability is to learn to listen to and act upon your intuition.

2 Listening to Your Intuition
Our minds don't have all the answers. Life is not just a rational process, our intuition is also involved (most women

know how true this is, most men are not so sure!). Can you trust your intuition? Do you know where to look for it? You are tapping into your intuition when you have a 'hunch' about something, when you know something to be true even if you haven't been told about it, you just *know*.

Sit quietly in a comfortable place and take some deep breaths. Relax your body and your mind. Focus your thoughts on your intuition.

- What feelings do you associate with your intuition?
- Are these feelings welcome of fearful (or anything else)?
- Think of three times that you have followed your intuition and things turned out well.
- Write down three things that your intuitive voice has been urging you to do. These might be only small things (for example 'write that letter' or 'read that book') or they might be about bigger issues (for example, 'move house', 'end that relationship').
- Why have you not acted on the advice of your intuition?

Your intuition gives you important information and speaks to you through urges, feelings and flashes of insight and the more you use it the more information it will give you. To hear your intuition you need to listen to your inner world of thoughts and feelings. Your intuition will always draw you to things that give you energy and encourage your creativity. Perhaps you have a great desire to change your life in some way but keep creating excuses which stop you putting your plans into action. Maybe you are afraid to follow your intuition because it involves change and a certain amount of risk taking. You can never trust yourself if you are denying the voice of your intuition: your levels of self-belief and self-respect will be low and so you will find it hard to trust the rest of the universe.

3 Contacting Your Intuition

Take some time every day, even if only for a few minutes, to contact and listen to your intuition. Find a quiet spot where you won't be interrupted, close your eyes and relax your body. Take some deep breaths and relax your mind.

In this relaxed and quiet state you can allow your intuition to come through. Give up one of your problems to your intuition and ask for help in finding an answer. You may immediately recognize your intuitive voice or you may not: everyone tunes into their inner self in a different way. You might experience strong feelings or you might not. You may have a flash of insight or you may have to wait until later. I often find that my intuition answers my questions when I am doing a very ordinary task like washing up or cleaning the floor! So be patient but keep practising daily. Eventually you will be able to tap into your intuition in any place at any time (practice makes perfect).

4 Making a Positive Affirmation

AFFIRMATION: *I trust my intuition.*

Say this to yourself whenever you remember. Write it on a piece of card and stick it somewhere where you see it all the time. Change those negative beliefs that say that your intuition doesn't exist or that you can't trust yourself to know the truth. The answers to your problems lie within you. Trust yourself, you have everything to gain.

Believe in yourself and others will believe in you. Learn to trust yourself and the rest of your world and you will feel utterly safe and totally supported. Listen to, develop and use your most powerful feminine instinct, your intuition –

all the answers you need can be found within you. You are a wise and powerful woman!

KEY POWER POINTS

These key points are here to remind you of why you are doing your *Trusting Yourself and Others* workouts. Refer to this list for constant encouragement and support. Reclaim the power that is yours!

1 Self-belief is the key ingredient of a happy and successful life.
2 Your levels of self-belief depend upon how much you trust yourself and others.
3 You were born totally trusting and full of belief in yourself and your world. Nothing has taken away these good feelings: the only change lies in your own perceptions.
4 Setbacks and change can often affect your levels of trust: everyone struggles with this problem. When trust levels are low it is easy to imagine that you alone are facing difficulties. This isn't true, we all have our lessons to learn.
5 You learned most of your ways of thinking about yourself and your world when you were a very small girl. If your upbringing was supportive you will have a deep, fundamental sense of trust which will help you through the bad times. If your very early childhood was unstable in some way it is likely to have had a negative effect on your levels of trust and self-belief.
6 The good news is that your beliefs can be changed! You can learn to trust. You can learn to believe in yourself.
7 Develop a close relationship with your intuition. You

have all the answers you will ever need deep inside you: just ask, trust and act on your wise inner voice.

8   When you act upon your intuition your energy levels and creative output will increase dramatically. What are you waiting for?

9   Be patient. Your intuition may not respond immediately and the answers might come in unexpected ways, so be prepared.

10 Learn to trust yourself and your world will become a safe and beautiful place.

12 Having Sexual Confidence

I don't think you have to be comfortable with a guy to be sexually confident – it's more important to be comfortable with yourself.

Pamela Hearne

- If you are feeling uncomfortable with your sexuality.
- When an intimate relationship has ended badly.
- When you just don't feel sexy.
- If you are worried about your body shape.
- If you feel sexually inexperienced.
- If you think that you are too old to be noticed any more.
- If you have a poor body image.
- If you are always 'too tired' for sex.

Women of all ages suffer from lack of sexual confidence: we are too young and inexperienced and may not be doing it right; we are too fat and uninteresting; we are too old ... add your own reasons to this list. The most important point here is that lack of sexual confidence is a common syndrome. Everywhere we look there are sexual images being used to sell things: cars, fast food, make-up, clothes, washing powder, paint, dog food and any other product you can think of. Sex sells! TV programmes, films, even the magazines we pick up in the dentist's waiting room bombard us with sexual images of magnificent young bodies with perfect complexions, snow-white teeth and gorgeous hair. *No wonder we struggle with sexual confidence.*

The glossy images which pervade our everyday lives are unreal. We know this to be true and yet we still buy into the myth of attaining physical perfection. It's great to keep up with fashion and try the latest make-up and skin-care products as long as we keep this all in perspective. Looking good and having a positive body image is all part of being a confident woman who knows herself and is proud of her body and is sexually confident.

On days when we find it hard to appreciate our unique bodies (we are premenstrual, menopausal, it's a bad hair day, the man in our life walked out, that piece of work just isn't coming together, our waistband is too tight, we are low in self-esteem, we didn't get much sleep, the children are playing up, we can't stop eating chocolate ... etc) we will feel low in the attraction stakes and our sexual confidence will be at level zero. What can we do to remain sexually confident in the face of all the images of perfection when we are feeling so far from perfect?

HOW TO HAVE SEXUAL CONFIDENCE

Workouts 1 and 2 look at how to maintain a good body image and what you need to do to get your body into optimum health and shape so that you increase your zest and vitality. Knowing what you want is a powerful aphrodisiac and Workout 3 shows you how to be more sure of yourself. Workout 4 looks at relationship issues and the important role that sex can play in your intimate life.

1 Maintaining a Good Body Image

Having a good body image and sexual confidence depends very much on *why* you want to develop these things. It is important to ensure that we are optimizing our assets so that we look good and feel good primarily for our own satisfaction. If we are motivated to make the best of ourselves because we feel that we are in sexual competition with each other to attract the attention of men, then we will never be sexually confident (there will always be someone more gorgeous, younger, thinner, curvier … etc). Maintain a good image by taking the following steps.

- Learn to love and appreciate your body, whatever its shape and size. This is the most important step; without this basic appreciation you will never be satisfied with yourself. Confidence is sexy so watch your posture, lift your head high and walk with pride.
- Make a list of your best features and emphasize them. If your legs are curvaceous, show them! If your hands are beautiful have them manicured regularly. Loving your body makes you feel gorgeous!
- Make sure that you take care of your hair and have a really good cut every few weeks. The state of our hair has a dramatic effect on how we feel about ourselves.
- Make the following affirmation as you go about your daily business:

AFFIRMATION: *I love my body.*

You might find this difficult especially on a low day, but say it even more on a low day as that's when you need it most! Loving your body gives you a sexy glow!

- If using certain beauty products makes you feel special then use them.
- Wear clothes that suit you in colours that are flattering. Don't be tempted to buy something that doesn't suit you just because it's fashionable as you will never feel happy and relaxed when you wear it. Looking and feeling relaxed is a vital element of looking good and feeling sexually confident.

Respect and love your body enough to make the very best of yourself. You are worth this attention and you will feel great! Have you noticed that when you are feeling good about yourself you attract other people to you? When you love yourself others will love you too!

2 Increasing Your Zest and Vitality

When your body is feeling good it looks good! High energy is a very attractive quality and it makes you feel fabulous.

Only you can know if you are fit or not and it's never too late to increase your fitness. If you need more exercise then decide to take it. Don't set yourself impossible workouts, you don't need to run ten miles a day! Start with something simple like going for a swim regularly and build this up gradually. Get on your bike. You don't *have* to go everywhere by car do you? Increase your exercise quotient and you will feel like a new woman.

Make sure that your diet is good. A diet of junk food will leave you feeling wrecked, stressed and lacking in sexual confidence. You know what you should and should not be eating: do your body a favour and give it the fuel that it needs for optimum functioning. Good food makes you feel good and look good.

3 Being Sure of Yourself

Self-confidence is the best aphrodisiac of all: the people we find most attractive have an air of knowing what they want about them. Your sexual confidence depends on your general confidence levels. If you are feeling unsure in any area of your life this will be reflected in your body image and you will look and feel sexually insecure. When your confidence falls there are a number of effective workouts you can use to help increase your self-belief (see the chapter

Becoming Confident on page 23). Another very effective approach is to focus on your area of insecurity (relationship, career, family or whatever) and ask this question: *'Am I being true to myself?'*

Sometimes we are not entirely truthful with ourselves. Perhaps we find it difficult to accept the truth and so we deny it. Take the problem area and start to understand it by asking the following questions:

- Am I being true to myself?
- If not, then why not?
- Am I trying to please someone?
- If so, why?
- Am I afraid to say 'no' to this person?
- What is the worst thing that can happen to me if I stand up for myself and do what I want to do?
- What is it that I want to do?

Investigate your areas of insecurity and stop living a lie. Be true to yourself and your confidence levels will soar (and so will your sexual confidence).

4 Having Healthy Intimate Relationships

If your sexual confidence is low within your intimate relationships it might be because of the type of people you are attracting and the way that you are behaving. Look at chapter 7, *Checking Your Relationships – Are They Healthy?* on page 47.

The definition of a healthy relationship is one where you are free to be yourself. If you are having an intimate relationship at present ask yourself this question: 'Am I feeling free to be me?' Check your boundary lines. Do you need to draw a new line in the sand? Are you afraid to say 'no' to your lover? Are either of you using sex as a bargaining tool? For example, do either of you say or imply that, 'If you take me there/buy me this/do that for me/behave the way I want you to, we will have sex. If not, I will withhold my sexuality.' Ask yourself why you are letting these things happen. What can you do to change them?

If you chase physical perfection and compare yourself with glossy young women in the media you will never have sexual confidence. If you think that you are in competition with other women for the attention of men then you are focusing in the wrong direction. Sexual confidence is about feeling comfortable with your body, your emotions and your mind. Learn to love your body, even the bits you don't find very attractive (especially these bits!). Treat your body well, it's the only one you have. Give it exercise and good nutrition and you will soon see and feel the difference. Self-confidence is the finest aphrodisiac of all. Know yourself, know what you want and don't be afraid to ask for it. Don't involve yourself in emotional games where sex is treated like a reward for good behaviour. When you feel free to be yourself your natural self-confidence and sexual confidence will shine through

KEY POWER POINTS

These key points are here to remind you of why you are doing your *Having Sexual Confidence* workouts. Refer to this list for constant encouragement and support. Reclaim the power that is yours.

1   Lack of sexual confidence is a common syndrome, you are not alone.

2 Optimize your assets so that you look and feel good for your *own* satisfaction. Being comfortable with yourself is one of the keys to sexual confidence.

3 Love and appreciate your body, whatever its shape and size. Loving your body makes you feel gorgeous.

4 Confidence is sexy so watch your posture, lift your head high and walk with pride.

5 Make the best of yourself – you are worth it!

6 Get physical and feel the benefit of a well-exercised and toned body.

7 Eat well and do your body a favour. Good food makes you feel good and look good.

8 Self-confidence is a powerful aphrodisiac. Work on your general confidence levels and your sexual confidence will improve.

9 Don't involve yourself in emotional games, where sex is used as a reward for good behaviour and withheld as a punishment.

10 Sexual confidence is all about feeling comfortable with your own body, mind and spirit. Know yourself, love yourself and accept yourself (warts and all).

13 Getting Men to Talk

Men use language to convey information and data. Women use language to form emotional bonds.

Janet Reibstein

- When your relationship is not working.
- When you feel that your partner doesn't understand you.
- If, in the middle of a row, he walks out to go and *do* something, leaving you emotionally frustrated.
- If your relationship has lost its sparkle.
- Whenever you feel that men and women are truly from different planets.
- When you are a victim in your intimate relationship.
- If you have stopped talking to each other.

Recently a women's magazine in the UK ran a survey asking readers what single thing would most improve the quality of their lives. Sixty per cent of women replied that all they wanted was for their partner to spend just 15 minutes a day talking to them 'meaningfully'. This doesn't seem to be asking much does it? But in the light of some other recent research we could well believe that it is. Women speak an average of 23,000 words a day whilst men only achieve an average of 12,000. We can't possibly be surprised by the figures: our own experience will confirm them.

Further research has shown that, whilst women automatically direct emotions to a part of the brain which enables them to talk about their feelings, men channel their emotions into actions rather than language. No surprises here either! How many times have you had a good row rudely interrupted by your man upping and leaving (to go to the pub, to meet his mates, to just drive around, to just *do* something) whilst you are in full flow?

Some of us might even think that this figure of 12,000 is rather optimistic! If you fall for the strong and silent type you are going to have to give him lots of support to help him to express his feelings. Be patient and stick with these workouts, the results will be worth it!

HOW TO GET MEN TO TALK

These workouts are designed to introduce new techniques and strategies into your communications with men. Do keep in mind at all times that men are indeed different from women: would you really want your man to talk like a woman? Don't try too hard to force open and emotional communications with a man. Start with small steps so that he can get used to the changes you are introducing into the relationship. Remember too that old habits die hard and if you want to get him to talk you will be asking him to break the habits of a lifetime. Workout 5 addresses this well: help to break this male lack of communication pattern by teaching your sons to talk about their feelings and to listen and relate sensitively to others. Your sons will one day appreciate this and so will their partners!

1 Organizing Talking Time

Be subtle in your approach. Remember that the results you want will be worth the effort that you put into your approach and surely your relationship is worth it! Rather than saying things like, 'You never talk to me', or 'We should be talking more', or 'Why don't you ever tell me what you are feeling?' or even 'Let's plan some time when we can talk to each other', try a more discreet method. Organize your schedule so that you are alone in a situation which makes it easy to talk. Do you remember how you used to 'date' in the early days when there was so much to talk about? Recreate this atmosphere. Go for a meal, go for a walk, get away from the TV and the internet! If you have children, organize a babysitter. If you can't get out of the house, plan a quiet evening with no electronic diversions. Be attentive (this always works like a dream!) and start by talking about his activities (this can lead to greater things).

Don't expect too much the first time you do this and refrain from explaining what you are trying to do. Create this new intimacy habit and he will get to like it (men like attention too!).

2 Letting Him Talk

Once he starts talking, *let him talk!* This may sound obvious but it is easy for women to slip into what's called an 'overlapping' mode. This is what we do when we are empathizing with other women. Your friend reveals some situation which she found difficult to handle and you show your support by diving in with 'I know just what you mean, the same thing happened to me and ...' We talk to women like this all the time because personal disclosures bring us closer and are recognized amongst women as being emotionally supportive. Beware! *Men can't stand this approach*, they don't understand the mechanics of such communication. So don't jump in there, when you are most tempted. If you do it will silence him.

Try to talk less than you usually do. We often find ourselves talking for a silent partner, filling in quiet spaces and maybe saying too much and regretting it. If there is silence let it be. If you want him to talk more there must be some silent spaces for him to talk into! This is hard. Resist all temptation to make a situation feel more comfortable by filling it with words. Sometimes silence is golden and a shared golden moment may be worth all the words he could possibly utter.

Listen well! Actively listen with all parts of yourself, your mind, body, spirit and emotions. Active listening produces an amazing communication bond. The person being listened to feels that he is valued and that his views are respected. Trust and further disclosure will develop from this approach. Listening in this way will keep you focused and will stop any tendency to overtalk.

3 Giving Constructive Feedback

One of the surest ways to wreck vocal communication is to criticize someone (this applies to men and women). The time when you are in conflict with your partner is probably the most important time to keep open the lines of communication so that you can both keep talking. When you are talking you are both trying to make the relationship work, when the talking stops you have given up!

Use this brilliant technique at times of conflict so that you can both *keep talking*.

However great the desire to yell and blame your partner – don't! As soon as you blame him you both enter the war zone and all effective communication will end! However 'right' you feel you are, remember the outcome that you want. Do you want to criticize and shout and have your partner walk out to *do* something? If this will give you the greatest satisfaction then go ahead and yell. But if you want to change his behaviour then realize that this approach will not work. Take a very deep breath and don't blame: use constructive criticism instead and open the talking lines! Here are some examples of the difference between criticizing and giving constructive feedback.

EXAMPLE
He's late for an important date with you.
The critical response: You annoy me when you don't arrive on time. You should be more together and stop wasting my time.
Constructive feedback response: When you don't turn up on time I feel frustrated because I've had to organize all sorts of things to get here on time.

EXAMPLE
He's not helping with the household chores.
The critical response: You're always taking me for granted and expecting me to do all the domestic work when you should be doing your share.
Constructive feedback response: When you don't help with the housework I feel used and taken for granted.

EXAMPLE
He isn't cuddling and hugging you enough.
The critical response: You never give me a cuddle when I need one and you make me feel neglected and unloved.
Constructive feedback response: When you forget to give me cuddles I feel uncared for.

For a good result you need to use the 'When you do that I feel like this' approach. Own your own feelings, stop blaming and allow the lines of communication to stay open between you. Some people will resist change and however

93

much you may work at acknowledging your own feelings they will find it impossible to do so. These people are blamers and if your man is one ask yourself this question 'Is he worth it'?

4 Keeping Some Things to Yourself

The desire to initiate conversation can make us talk too much: when we try to fill in the quiet spaces between us and our partner we can easily get a dose of verbal diarrhoea and disclose too much. Self-revelation is a good communication tool and encourages others to disclose personal information. Women use this technique all the time: I tell you something personal about me and then you return the favour and our level of intimacy deepens. Men are much less inclined to use this tactic and some don't understand its purpose. If the man in question is not returning the favour and we just keep revealing more and more, then we can easily end up telling more than is good for us and boring the man. Enjoy the satisfaction of keeping some things to yourself, maintain some mystery, don't tell him absolutely every minute detail of your day. Some things are best kept for your women friends; some things are best kept to yourself.

5 Teaching Your Sons to Talk

If you have a son you can teach him to be sensitive to the feelings of others, to listen well and to talk about his emotions. This is not hard to do, young boys are keen to use these communication skills and grow into young men who know how to talk to women. Your son will thank you for this talent and you will be helping to break a pattern of poor male communication skills. Men *can* talk to women, they just need to know how!

Most men can be encouraged to talk more and to become increasingly aware of their own (and your) emotions. If this is the outcome that you want then be prepared to be subtle and yet focused on your approach. Remember, *you* are the expert and he is learning new skills. If, after countless patient hours on your part, he still fails to respond then you must ask yourself if he is really worth all the effort. When he becomes responsive don't expect everything at once. If you take it easy, one step at a time, the results can be amazing.

KEY POWER POINTS

These key points are here to remind you of why you are doing your *Getting Men to Talk* workouts. Refer to this list for constant encouragement and support. Reclaim the power that is yours!

1   Men and women communicate differently! Men speak to give information and women speak to create emotional bonds. Always keep this in mind.
2   Women are physically more capable of understanding and talking about their feelings. Men channel their emotions into actions.
3   You are trying to get him to change a lifetime habit so go slowly and be patient.
4   Recreate your dating days: think of all the fascinating chats you used to have and have them again.
5   Make time to talk. Do this discreetly; turn off all electronic screens and *be attentive* (he will love this!).
6   When he gets going *let him talk*. Resist all temptation to interrupt.
7   Sometimes silence is golden.

8   Listen well. This will help to develop trust and further disclosure.
9   Own your own feelings and stop blaming him. Constructive feedback will keep the lines of communication open.
10 Teach your sons to be good communicators; the world will be a better place.

14 Forgiving Yourself and Others

The magic of forgiveness cannot be explained: it can only be experienced. Go ahead and experience it!

- If you can't stop feeling angry with someone.
- When you feel guilty.
- If it's hard for you to express your feelings.
- When you don't know what you feel.
- If you just can't seem to let go of some thing, situation or person.
- When you hate yourself.
- If you are low in self-respect.
- Whenever you find yourself blaming someone else for your own problems.
- Whenever you feel as if you are stuck in the past.

Forgiveness is a powerful way of increasing our personal power. When I first suggest to people that they might forgive someone who makes them angry, they usually say, 'Why should I after what they have done to me?' Forgiveness does not mean that we think it's OK for anybody to do anything to us. Forgiveness is all about letting go. If I can't forgive you then my angry thoughts will connect me with you forever. You may live ten thousand miles away, but if all I have to do is think of you and my emotions are all stirred up then I might as well be living with you. And so it is that we can be bound in hatred all our lives to people who we may never even see. We may even be carrying anger for someone who has died (this is not at all unusual). When we can't forgive (let go) we surely reach the heights of self-victimization!

Is there someone you find it difficult to forgive? If so, ask yourself what you gain from not forgiving them. You gain a permanent relationship with this person: you are bound together by anger. Is this what you really want?

HOW TO FORGIVE YOURSELF AND OTHERS

Workout 1 examines the process of forgiveness and Workouts 2 and 3 demonstrate different techniques that you can use to help you to let go. Of course we will always find that the hardest person to forgive is ourselves (we are constantly self-critical): Workout 4 explains the power of self-forgiveness.

1 Understanding the Process of Forgiveness

Forgiving does not mean overlooking, it means the opposite. Before you can let go of the ties that bind you to another person in hatred, you need to know exactly what hurt you and why it hurt you and then you need to express this in an appropriate way.

1 Name the person who you are trying to forgive.

. . . .

2 What exactly did they do that hurt you so much?

. . . .

3 Why was this action so painful for you?

. . . .

4 Find some way to express this appropriately. Do you need to tell this person how you feel? Would it help?

Perhaps it would be enough to talk this through with a friend. Do you need professional help? Maybe you just need to write down your feelings and then burn the paper. Take whatever course of action you need to acknowledge your pain.

5   Once you can recognize and accept your pain you can give it up and let go: forgive, let go and set yourself free.

2 Visualizing – The Last Day on Earth Forgiveness
Choose the person you find it most difficult to forgive.

Find a quiet place, sit comfortably and relax. Close your eyes and become aware of your breathing. If your thoughts crowd your mind, just go back to concentrating on your breathing. When you are ready, bring to mind your chosen person. You can see this person in front of you and you know that it is their last day on earth. You will never see this person again. What would you like to say to them? If you feel like shouting, then do it. If you feel like crying, then do it. This is your big chance to clear up your relationship. You become aware that this person also wants to resolve the situation. He/she is listening closely to all that you have to say. When you have finished, let the other person speak. What are they saying? How do they see your relationship? When the communication between you is over, hear yourself forgiving this person. Hold the picture of them in your mind and say out loud, 'I forgive you'.

Open your eyes and congratulate yourself on a magnificent effort. Forgiveness is hard work because it takes us deep into our old behaviour patterns where we have to deal with heavy emotional issues. We can only forgive bit by bit and so you may have to repeat this visualization many times over a period of time. Just when you think you have finally forgiven, up it all pops again –

Christmas family reunions often provide the setting. If this happens, don't give up. Continue with the visualization.

The most important thing to remember is that every tiny scrap of forgiveness that you can find in your heart will move mountains of emotional pain. Use this visualization for anybody you need to forgive, dead or alive. The strong intention to forgive is really all you need; the rest will take care of itself. Try it and see!

3 Writing Your Forgiveness

Choose someone to forgive (there will be plenty to choose from). Take a large piece of paper and write on the first line:

I . . . . (your name), forgive you . . . . (their name).

Then do it again. Whenever you feel or think anything in particular as you are writing, turn the page over and write it down. Affirmations bring up your negativity; this is the way that they work. Don't be shocked by the things that you have written on the back of the paper. Remember you are letting go of these thoughts and feelings. Become aware of what is happening to you as you are doing your forgiveness. When you forgive someone in this way you are making a positive affirmation about your intention towards that person: the intention is that you are both going to be released from the bondage of unforgiveness. It may take a while before you experience any inner reaction to your forgiveness. Whatever does or does not appear to be happening, just keep on forgiving.

Write the affirmation 35 times a day for 10 days. Don't give up and don't keep looking for results: just keep writing the affirmation and keep writing the responses.

How do you feel after 10 days of forgiveness? What

feelings have you experienced? What have you discovered about yourself?

Forgiveness is a great discloser of the truth. If you keep forgiving, all will eventually be revealed – it becomes impossible to deceive yourself. You will become a woman who is free to love and value herself and this is truly a powerful place to be.

4 Forgiving Yourself

And who do we find hardest to forgive? Why, ourselves of course. We are our own hardest critics: can we ever be good enough, clever enough, talented enough …? (Enter your own favourites here.) When we are low in confidence we become our own worst enemy and as we heap on the self-criticism we enter a negative spiral which makes us feel worse and worse.

Self-forgiveness is the key to empowerment. When we can love and value ourselves, despite our shortcomings, we become free to be ourselves and to reach our highest potential. Break the critical habit which is such a waste of your precious time.

- When you start to criticize yourself, become aware of what you are doing and stop!
- Say '*I forgive myself*'. Use this as an affirmation and say it as often as possible – sing it in the bath/in the car/at the bus stop (under your breath).
- Ask yourself these questions:
  What did I do that was so terrible?
  Haven't I blamed myself enough?
  Has blaming myself done any good?
- Let go of self-blame, forgive yourself, free yourself.

Whenever you hang on to old, hurtful memories your life becomes slow, stuck, routinized and boring. Anger and disempowerment go hand in hand. Stop living in the past or it will ruin your life. Stop reacting and start acting. Undo your painful past by giving up and letting go of the hurt and your future will be clearer, lighter and brighter.

KEY POWER POINTS

These key points are here to remind you of why you are doing your *Forgiving Yourself and Others* workouts. Refer to this list for constant encouragement and support. Reclaim the power that is yours!

1 Forgiveness is a powerful way of increasing your personal power.
2 When you can't let go (forgive) you reach the heights of self-victimization.
3 When we forgive someone we are *never* condoning their behaviour: we are saying that what they did was unacceptable – forgiveness starts with this realization.
4 You only need to recognize and accept your painful memories and then you can let them go.
5 You are a powerful woman and you can let go of anything which holds you back from achieving your own true potential.
6 Forgiveness is a great discloser of the truth: keep forgiving and eventually all will be revealed.
7 Each small act of forgiveness will move mountains of emotional pain. Keep forgiving even if feels like you are getting nowhere. Trust that you are.
8 You are your own hardest critic. Break the critical habit and it will transform your life.
9 Let go of blame, forgive others, forgive yourself, free yourself!

15 Being a 'Good Enough' Mother

How is it that mothers can be regarded by so many people as both angel and villain, chaste vessel of purity and whore, queen of wisdom and consummate idiot?

Claire Rayner

- If you ever feel guilty in your mothering role.
- When you have nothing left to give any member of your needy family.
- If you feel that you have lost a part of yourself to your child.
- When you feel that you are not a 'good enough' mother.
- Whenever you feel resentment towards your children (Most common and absolutely normal!).
- If you feel like a victim to your family.
- When the boundary lines keep changing and you don't know which rules will work any more.
- When you don't *always* feel overwhelming love for your child.

Whether you are a mother, have chosen not to be, or cannot have children, the concept of motherhood will be one which you have wrestled with. We all share the experience of some powerfully strong (and not necessarily true) cultural beliefs which contain variations on the following themes.

- Mothers love their children.
- Women are born to be mothers.

- Motherhood is natural and easy.
- Mother knows best.
- Motherhood is bliss.
- Motherhood is instinctive.

What sort of things did you believe about motherhood before you had your baby?

If the hand that rocks the cradle rules the world how come most mothers spend so much time feeling disempowered? As the images of the radiant earth mother and powerful matriarch fade into more mundane and domestic forms we begin a new and complex relationship with our child and with ourselves in our new (and unpractised) role. We find ourselves in a job for which we have no experience (except our own experience of being mothered). Modern society isolates us in a new and exhausting role with no time off, no holidays and no pay: it is difficult not to be stretched by these conditions sometimes!

Having a baby is a fantastic experience and brings with it so many intense emotions. This fast-moving and ever-changing experience never seems to settle into a recognizable and controllable routine, but once we reconcile ourselves to this emotional roller-coaster we can learn to sit back and enjoy the ride. Guilt and motherhood are often close relations: this relationship can ruin your experience of being a mother. Don't let it! We can only ever do our best and that is 'good enough'.

HOW TO BE A 'GOOD ENOUGH' MOTHER

Workout 1 shows how to assess the quality of your mothering and helps you to answer the question, 'Am I doing a good job as a mother?' Workout 2 looks at our mothering patterns by linking the two experiences of being a daughter and being a mother. Workout 3 is a checklist to hang on your wall to help you to remember to honour the act of motherhood and respect yourself for undertaking such a challenging job.

1 Not Being Victimized

How can you tell if you are always doing your best for your children? Given the complexities of the job and the intense emotions involved, the best indicator is always yourself. If you are feeling high in self-esteem your judgement will be sound: if you are low in self-esteem your decision-making will be ineffective and your actions inconsistent. When you are feeling low self-esteem in your mothering role you are allowing yourself to be victimized by your family. Victim consciousness denotes the need for a change in mothering behaviour. Teenagers are particularly good at pushing our victim buttons.

'Oh, why can't I go, all the others are going?'
'I really need to take the car tonight, otherwise I will miss this really important (whatever).'
'There's no point going if I can't stay out until ... All the others are allowed.'

And so they go on, always trying to change the rules and widen the boundaries, day after day it sometimes seems. Each time you are confronted by your children in this way, ask yourself this question: 'If I say yes, how will I feel?'

If you feel unsure, worried and low in self-esteem you are allowing yourself to be victimized. Support your own instincts, learn to say 'no' and investigate what is going on.

(What about all these 'others'? A quick phone call to the parents of these other children will often reveal a different story than the one that you have been told.)

Don't ever be afraid to be an assertive mother; your children can only benefit. Don't allow your children to victimize you: it is in neither their best interest nor yours. Your children will only respect you if you respect yourself. Remember that our children do what we do and not what we say. High and low self-esteem are contagious and your children will catch whatever variety you have. Work on yourself and all the rest will follow. Recognize and accept any feelings of guilt, anger, resentment etc (yes, mothers are human too!), and then you can let these feelings go and move on to clear assertive decision-making and action-taking. Children need good, strong guidelines and they expect them from you. They respond to positive action and supportive parenting which enhances their self-esteem and yours.

2 Being a Daughter and Being a Mother

We are the mothers we have learned to be.

We learned our deep beliefs about mothering when we were baby daughters, and we learned them from our mothers. We can make a direct link with the behaviour patterns we have learned and the ones that we are now teaching our own children.

STEP 1 Exercise: Memories of my mother
You will need a notebook and pen.

Go back as far as you can into your childhood to answer these questions. It might be helpful to look at some photos of yourself and your mother taken in those early days. Perhaps you can remember some specific outings, holidays or events that will help you to focus your memories. If you can talk to your mother about your babyhood, so much the better.

1 Was your mother very emotional during your childhood? Yes/No
2 If the answer is 'yes', describe her emotions and the way that she showed them.
3 Was your mother able to show her love for you? Yes/No
4 If 'yes', describe the ways that she demonstrated her love – if 'no', say why you think she could not show you her love.
5 Describe how you are feeling now, as you are doing this exercise.
6 Do you think that your mother enjoyed looking after you when you were a child? Yes/No
7 Explain why you think she did or did not enjoy looking after you.
8 How would you describe the relationship between your parents when you were small? In which ways do you think they were supportive or not supportive of each other?
9 How would you describe your mother's level of self-esteem when you were a little girl? (If you can ask her now how she felt it might be helpful.)
10 Why do you think that she felt this way?
11 Describe your relationship with your mother now. (If she is dead you can still answer because you will always have a relationship with your mother.)

Some of you may have found this exercise very painful.

Mother and child relationships are always potentially highly charged emotionally. We begin this emotional roller-coaster ride as soon as we are born: when we ourselves become mothers, we take a front seat and the speed accelerates.

Put your answers aside for a moment and follow Step 2.

STEP 2 Exercise: Me as a mother

In this exercise we change roles, from daughter to mother.

1 Are you able to show your emotions to your children? Yes/No
2 If not, why not? If you are able to show your emotions how do you do this?
3 Do you find it easy to show physical affection for your children? Yes/No
4 In what ways do you show your love for your children?
5 Do you ever wish that you had not had your children? Yes/No
6 How would you describe the relationship between you and the father of your children?
7 How do you think your role as a mother affects your levels of self-esteem?
8 Describe your relationship with your own children now.

Compare your two sets of answers. Are there any connecting links? As we unravel our learned patterns it is important to remember that our mothers had mothers too! We can rant and rave at our own mother's mistakes and then, before we know it, the roles have changed and our children are looking at us. If we cannot forgive our mothers for their mistakes we cannot forgive our own. Let go of blame and use the information from this workout to clarify your own patterns. Recognize your mother's patterns; recognize your own; change the ones that don't work and your children will be free to change. We pass on our patterns to our children, let them be patterns of high self-esteem.

3 Honouring Motherhood

Being a mother is a most challenging/amazing/fascinating/ frightening/thrilling job! Sometimes it's easy to let ourselves be taken for granted and whenever we do this we diminish the importance of motherhood. Copy out the following list and hang it somewhere prominent so that you *never* forget to honour motherhood.

- Motherhood is a *big* job.
- I am a good mother. I am doing my best.
- Motherhood is vital – the survival of the race depends on it.
- Guilt is not an intrinsic part of motherhood. I don't *have* to feel guilty.
- When guilt engulfs me, I can just step out of it. Guilt ruins family life.
- I need to look after myself. I cannot give to others if I have nothing left to give.
- There are no perfect mothers; we all make lots of mistakes. It's OK to make mistakes; this is how we learn.
- I am free to feel and to express all of my emotions.
- Motherhood is a state of potential conflict. I can accept this and work with it. I am flexible and creative.
- My children do what I do and not what I say.
- I forgive and thank my mother. She taught me what she knew about mothering.
- It is safe for my children to grow up. I can easily let them go.

- I pass on my patterns of self-esteem to my children. I can create high self-esteem.
- I deserve a supportive and validating family life.

Motherhood is not easy and instinctive. Don't expect yourself to be the perfect mother all the time (or even any of the time). This is the most challenging job you will ever face so get it in perspective right from the beginning. You will make mistakes, just let them go and learn from them; move on, don't trap yourself with guilt. A mother who can make clear and consistent boundary lines for her children will be able to enjoy the job of mothering. Remember that you pass on your patterns of self-esteem to your children – let those patterns be upbeat and positive.

KEY POWER POINTS

These key points are here to remind you of why you are doing your *Being a 'Good Enough' Mother* workouts. Refer to this list for constant encouragement and support. Reclaim the power that is yours!

1 Guilt and motherhood are often closely linked; don't let guilt ruin your precious experiences of being a mother.
2 We can only ever do our best and that is 'good enough'.
3 Don't ever let yourself be victimized by your loved ones. Be an assertive mother, this is the best example that you can give your children.
4 We are the mothers we have learned to be. Thank and forgive your mother, she taught you what she had been taught.
5 Always honour and respect the act of motherhood,

never diminish its importance: the hand that rocks the cradle rules the world.

6 Accept that motherhood is always a state of potential conflict: you can work with this by remaining flexible and imaginative.

7 Your children do what you do, not what you say, so walk your talk.

8 It is safe for us all to grow up. Practise letting go in small ways even when your children are quite small. Mothers need to learn how to let go!

9 You can create high self-esteem and pass this pattern on to your children.

10 You *are* a good enough mother!

Healing

16 Letting Go of Addictions

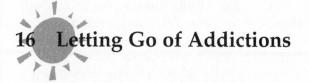

... men may not be the only thing we're hooked on. In order to block our deepest feelings from childhood, some of us have also developed dependencies on addictive substances.

Robin Norwood

- If you act compulsively in ways that punish yourself and numb your pain.
- If you are trying to change a man.
- If you are in an abusive relationship.
- If you feel a sense of shame.
- If you have secrets that you feel you can't possibly share.
- If you hate yourself.
- If you are having a relationship with a man who is no good for you.
- If you were brought up in a family where feelings were not expressed, needs were not recognized and behaviour was critical and invalidating.

An addiction appears to be life-enhancing, but is really soul-destroying. Addictive behaviour is rooted in self-hate, and an addicted person has very low self-esteem. Many women are involved in some form of addictive behaviour to compensate for the fact that we have lost touch with our own truth and that now it is too painful for us to recognize our own emotional needs.

Perhaps you are wondering if you have any addictions. We can be addicted to men who are 'needy'. We may attract abusive relationships, overeat, undereat, drink too much, workout too much, take drugs (illegal or prescribed), indulge in compulsive sex, shoplift, overspend, overwork, smoke, gamble ... if we are compulsively using any behaviour to hide from ourselves, then we are addicted.

Let's return to the cradle where all our stories begin. Women with addictions were little girls from troubled families. Two people in a damaging, intimate love relationship can create a troubled family. A damaging relationship runs on the following principles.

- Needs are not recognized or met.
- Feelings are not expressed.
- Behaviour is invalidating and critical.
- Low self-esteem prevails.

These negative thought, behaviour and feeling patterns undermine the child of such a relationship. She learns that she cannot trust her own instincts and perception and that the world is a frightening place. Small wonder if she grows up looking for a way to numb her pain! If you grew up amidst such negative patterning (as so many of us do) then it is highly likely that you will be involved in some form of addictive behaviour to compensate yourself, hide from yourself and punish yourself.

HOW TO LET GO OF ADDICTIONS

The first two workouts help you to throw some light on your addictive behaviour and on the secret behaviours which surround them. Workout 3 introduces a 5-step programme for change and Workout 4 offers some self-supporting affirmations.

1 Looking at Your Addictions

We can be addicted to chocolate, to abusive relationships with men, to sugar or to not eating. We can be addicted to shopping, to working out or even to not walking on the cracks in the pavement! There are so many ways we can be addicted to so many things. Some addictions are life threatening and others threaten the quality of our life. We cannot compare our addictions. Each case is unique, and only you can know how your behaviour is affecting your life. If you act compulsively in ways that punish yourself and numb your pain, you are addicted. Your addiction may be a secret, but please don't feel ashamed to answer these questions. Remember that most of us are from troubled families and nearly all of us have had or are having relationships with men who are no good for us (this is an addiction). Having several addictions is very common.

Answer the following questions.

* What are your addictions?

. . . .
* Are your addictions a secret? Yes/No
* If your addictions are secret, why are they?

. . . .
* How do you feel about your addictions?

. . . .
* Can you imagine life without your addictions?

. . . .
* Have you ever tried to break your addictions? Yes/No
* Would you like to break your addictive patterning? Yes/No

We become addicted because we are in emotional pain. The

117

addiction numbs the pain and so we are afraid to release the addiction. In order to do so you may need medical help or some other kind of professional help. You may need a counsellor and/or support group. When you are ready to change, you will not be afraid to ask for help. You will be amazed to find that many other people are acting out your 'secret' behaviours.

2 Looking at the Secret Behaviours Surrounding Your Addictions

Make a list of all the behaviours surrounding your addictions which you have never told anybody about. Perhaps you ate your child's chocolate, kept a stash of alcohol in the car, stole money to pay for your addiction, lied to your loved ones to protect your secret, smoked cigarette butts from the pavement or rubbish bin, drank salt water to make yourself sick after an eating binge ...

1 . . . .

2 . . . .

3 . . . .

What is your most terrible secret? Did you write it down?

Now forgive yourself. Visualize yourself enacting your very worst secret behaviour. Look at this picture of yourself in pain and say the following affirmation:

AFFIRMATION: *I love you and I forgive you.*

You are addicted because you are full of self-hate. Your addiction numbs the pain and punishes you further so your self-hate is reinforced. Your recovery begins with self-forgiveness.

3 Applying the 5-Step Programme for Change

When our addictions are in the spotlight we feel vulnerable. We would love to relieve the pressure by blaming something or someone, but of course this tactic does not work. As soon as we look outside ourselves for answers we become disempowered. When we make the important link between our addictive behaviour and the negative patterning of our early childhood, we start a powerful process. Because we have suppressed our power (and our anger) and numbed our pain for so long, the first sign of our empowerment is the return of angry feelings. (Our fear of our own anger can keep us in our addiction.) If you have an addiction, then you will also have a volcano of rage which will start to bubble as soon as you understand the negative patterning underlying your condition. Anger is only energy. As you move through the process of understanding and releasing your addictive behaviour, use this anger creatively: use it to motivate you and not to hurt others or yourself. Seek professional help and support if you need to.

As you work on accepting and letting go of your anger, your rage will diminish and you will become more assertive. As you reclaim your lost personal power, you will find that your self-esteem will rise and you will feel empowered to tackle the effects of negative patterning in your life. Your addictive behaviours (in relationships, with food, with drugs or whatever) can be changed.

THE 5-STEP PROGRAMME FOR CHANGE
Use the 5-Step Programme to evaluate your situation.

119

Healing

1 Assess the situation
Describe your relationship with your addiction.

. . . .

2 Decide what you would like to change
What don't you like about your condition? (Ignore negative thoughts about how it's too hard or impossible to change.)

. . . .

3 Specify your preferred outcome
How do you want things to change? Make assertive and specific statements. You *can* change, just believe it!

. . . .

4 Recognize the negative patterning involved
If you can do this, you are on your way. You are brave to have come this far.

. . . .

Deep self-hatred, the need to fill the emptiness inside, fear of anger, desire to be in control (ironic though it may seem), a need to punish yourself and a lack of self-forgiveness are some of the things that brought you here.

5 Change the negative patterns – re-pattern your life
We are all working on our negative thought and behaviour patterns in our search for greater personal awareness and empowerment. Viewed in this way, we are all addicts – we are addicted to repeating patterns. Your addiction might actually be life-threatening or it might have the potential to wreck your life in a different way. It is impossible to

compare the severity of addictions and their power to ruin lives. Each case is unique and only you know if you need professional assistance to help you to change your patterns. More and more people are recognizing their addictions and asking for help. There are numerous support groups available. Whatever your problem, remember that you are not alone. Go and find help if you need it.

You are a wonderfully brave and talented woman and all you really need is love – lots and lots of self-love.

4 Using Self-Supporting Affirmations

Whether you need outside support or not, to let go of your addictions you will always need your own support. As you say these affirmations, visualize their truth. See yourself free and happy, and make these visions as real as you can.

SELF-SUPPORTING AFFIRMATIONS:
I am free.
No person has any power over me.
Nothing has any power over me.
I am safe at all times.
I can trust my instincts.
I love myself.
I am decisive.
I can make things happen.

Try writing your affirmations. Choose one and write it 20 times on one side of paper. If your negativity surfaces (as eventually it will if you repeat this exercise enough), write your negative thoughts on the other side of the paper. This is a powerful way to start releasing negativity. Don't give up on this exercise, it isn't just academic. Remember that positive affirmations can replace negative beliefs. Keep at it,

121

let go of your addictive behaviour – your reward is your personal freedom.

Addictions enchant us by appearing to enhance our lives and numb our pain: this is an illusion. Addictions enslave us, wreck our lives and keep us at rock bottom. Releasing addictions requires dedication, focus and high motivation, but the rewards are priceless. Forgive yourself, let go of blame and climb out of your negative patterning. You can do this!

NOTE: I have only been able to touch briefly on the subject of addictions here. If you would like more in-depth knowledge I recommend that you read Robin Norwood's brilliant book, *Women Who Love Too Much*.

KEY POWER POINTS

These key points are here to remind you of why you are doing your *Letting Go of Addictions* workouts. Refer to this list for constant encouragement and support. Reclaim the power that is yours!

1   An addiction appears to be life enhancing, but is really soul destroying.
2   Many women are involved in some form of addictive behaviour.
3   If you are compulsively using any behaviour to hide from your true feelings, then you are addicted.
4   Women with addictions were little girls from troubled families. If you grew up amongst negative patterns (as so many of us do) then it's highly likely that you will be involved in some form of addictive behaviour to

compensate yourself, hide from yourself and punish yourself. *You are not alone!*

5   Most women have had or are having a relationship with a man who is not good for them: this is a common addiction!

6   You may need professional support to help you to let go of your addiction. Don't be afraid to reach out to others. When you are ready to change you will not be afraid to ask for help.

7   Many other people are acting out your 'secret' behaviours.

8   Love yourself: your recovery begins with self-forgiveness.

9   Anger is only energy. Use it creatively and constructively, let it keep you motivated and determined.

10 No person and no thing has any power over you. You are free.

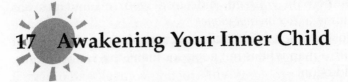

17 Awakening Your Inner Child

But trailing clouds of glory do we come ...

William Wordsworth

- When you are having problems trusting yourself and others.
- For difficulties in maintaining intimate personal relationships.
- When you are dealing with feelings of guilt and shame.
- When you need some fun in your life!

Look into a baby's eyes and see the joy and delight which can be found there. You were once like this: thrilled and enchanted by life and full of positive expectations. Whatever happened to that little girl who was so open and trusting and full of the wonder of life? She hasn't gone anywhere. Your enchanted (and enchanting) little girl is still there within you, buried somewhere and longing to be free.

Whenever we experience feelings of unworthiness (I'm just not good enough), guilt, shame or lack of trust, we can always trace these emotions back to our childhood, where we learned how to feel about ourselves and the rest of the universe. As tiny, vulnerable little girls, with wonder in our eyes, we quickly learned to fit into the agendas of our parents and the rest of society. To cope with our lives we learned to build defences to 'protect' ourselves from being let down and disappointed. We may have been hurt so deeply that this open and trusting part of ourselves has become totally buried and we can be said to have abandoned our Inner Child. This means that we have lost contact with that playful, loving and open part of ourselves.

If you have problems with trusting yourself and others, if you aren't enjoying your life, if you experience feelings of shame, guilt and unworthiness, then learning to awaken your Inner Child will be a powerful and life enhancing technique for you. Reawaken the girl within you and rediscover a world of delight and playfulness. Encourage your Inner Child to emerge and you will find that it will be easier to form close relationships and to trust others, to express your feelings, to feel much more optimistic and to have fun!

HOW TO AWAKEN YOUR INNER CHILD

Try the workouts below. Start with the technique which most appeals to you. Be gentle with yourself and if you feel emotional allow your feelings to express themselves (this is all part of the healing process). Don't try to do too much at once. Each of these techniques is very powerful, so little and often is probably the best approach. Prepare to be amazed.

1 Going Back to Your Childhood

We all have sensual experiences which can link us with our past. They may be smells, tastes, textures, noises, movements. Childhood memories can be rekindled by the touch of velvet, the taste of an acid drop, the smell of polish, the sound of the sea, a ride on a see-saw … Are there any sensual experiences which take you back to your childhood? Can you fill in any of the categories that follow?

Healing

Touch . . . .

Taste . . . .

Smell . . . .

Sound . . . .

Movement. . . . .

If you have discovered any experiences which remind you of your childhood then *recreate those experiences*. Go and eat a sherbert dip, watch a Magic Roundabout video, ride a donkey, blow some bubbles, run along the beach, play with marbles, go to the fair and smell the candyfloss, go on the dodgems and *eat* the candyfloss ... Your list may start very small, but the more you live these memories the more childhood pleasures you will start to remember.

2 Having Fun

List as many fun activities that you can think of which will help to reawaken your Inner Child. Think of things that a small child would enjoy, and then *you* do them.

Do at least one playful thing a day, *just for the fun of it*; the experience will grow on you.

3 Looking at Some Photographs

Find some photographs of yourself at various stages of your childhood. Put them in prominent positions around the house and look at them frequently. Get familiar with the way these children look. Make friends with these children and learn to love them as your very own: they *are* your very own. Each of these children is a part of you: reconnect with them and you will again assimilate all the amazing childlike qualities which you have lost in the process of 'growing up'.

4 Drawing a Picture with Crayons

This is such a powerful technique so please don't avoid it because you think you can't draw: this has nothing to do with creating a masterpiece. Take some crayons and a piece of paper and draw a picture of yourself as a child. Use the hand that you don't normally use. If you feel like it, go on and draw yourself as a child with your parents, and maybe the house where you lived. Carry on drawing if you are enjoying it. Stick your pictures up on the wall if you are brave enough. You might find yourself transported to your childhood by the mere smell of the crayons. Give this workout a try, you will be surprised by its effect.

Allow yourself to see the world through the clear eyes of a child. Free yourself to trust others. Let go of guilt, shame and feelings of unworthiness. Enjoy this life to the full.

KEY POWER POINTS

These key points are here to remind you of why you are doing your *Awakening Your Inner Child* workouts. Refer to this list for constant encouragement and support. Reclaim the power that is yours!

1 Your enchanted, trusting and joyful little girl is still within you, buried somewhere and longing to be released.
2 Let down your 'protective' defences: openness will set you free.
3 Feelings of shame, guilt and unworthiness will disempower you. Decide to let go of these feelings.
4 You deserve to have some fun. So have it!
5 Start to trust other people and they will start to trust you.

Healing

6 You get what you expect. Let your natural optimism shine through, you will be amazed at the results.
7 Allow yourself to express your feelings, it is an important part of your healing process.
8 Free your Inner Child and enjoy your life.
9 You are not alone. Women everywhere struggle with issues of unworthiness, guilt and shame. We are all in this together. Let this thought empower you.

18 Receiving Angelic Blessings

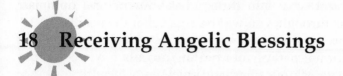

Angels, with their infinite love and compassion, are waiting to help us.

Diana Cooper

- When life loses its meaning.
- When shopping gets boring!
- Whenever you need to feel uplifted.
- If you need help.
- If your life feels empty.
- Whenever you lose trust: in yourself, in others or in the universe.
- When you long to experience a divine connection.
- If you feel depressed and low in energy.

We are entering a new Golden Age where the emphasis is on our spiritual development rather than on our material comforts. People are already seeking to enhance their own personal awareness. The material comforts of this world are only transitory, their end will come. Our human bodies will also turn to dust when our time on Earth ends. As we develop in consciousness we are becoming more and more aware of the spiritual dimension in our lives. People are realizing that money and the power that it brings do not automatically bring happiness, and so are becoming more concerned with the development of personal qualities within themselves which will bring peace, joy and contentment. We cannot buy such things as love, peace and happiness but we can receive these gifts if we allow ourselves to tap into the spiritual world and fulfil our divine connection.

Angels are always near you to offer help, support and guidance whenever you need it. You only have to ask, but ask you must. Your guardian angel has been with you since your birth: you are not alone on the planet! If you only knew how much help the angelic world can give you, you would never feel frightened and alone again. Suspend your disbelief for a short while; open your heart and just see what the universe can offer you.

HOW TO RECEIVE AN ANGELIC BLESSING

Set aside your disbelief and give yourself wholeheartedly to these workouts. If you do this, I can promise you that you will be amazed! Workout 1 shows you how to make a set of angelic blessing cards which will enable you to draw on the angelic essences you need. Workout 2 invites you to a meeting with your guardian angel. Workout 3 will prepare you to expect a miracle. Enjoy these workouts!

1 Making Your Angelic Blessing Cards

Transfer the words below on to paper or card, to make your own set of 30 angelic blessing cards. These cards provide key words that will help you to focus on particular aspects of your inner life.

SIMPLICITY	ENTHUSIASM	HEALING
FLEXIBILITY	SURRENDER	GRACE
SPONTANEITY	INSPIRATION	HONESTY
ADVENTURE	GRATITUDE	RESPONSIBILITY
HUMOUR	COURAGE	OPENNESS
TRUTH	WILLINGNESS	CLARITY

BEAUTY	HARMONY	CREATIVITY
COMPASSION	FORGIVENESS	TENDERNESS
FAITH	UNDERSTANDING	FREEDOM
LOVE	INTEGRITY	BALANCE

Find a quiet place and lay out your cards face down in front of you. Relax and close your eyes and then turn your attention to a particular problem for which you need help. Silently ask for divine assistance and as you do so you will feel your energy changing. When you are ready, choose a card. The card you choose is the angelic essence which you need to assimilate at this time. Close your eyes again and contemplate and absorb the qualities that this card brings. The angel who represents this essence will be with you as you go about your business. (I often take an angel to work with me in my pocket.) Think about the quality reflected by the card and as you do you will find this quality reflecting in all manner of ways throughout your day. Ask for an angelic blessing and choose a card whenever you feel the need. Strengthen your divine connection and amazing things will happen.

2 Meeting Your Guardian Angel

STEP 1
Find a quiet spot where you won't be disturbed. Sit down or lie down somewhere comfortable. Close your eyes and relax your body from your toes to your head; feel every part of you relaxing as your awareness travels up your body. Become aware that your breathing is slowing down and feel your mind relaxing as you become more centred.

STEP 2

Invite your guardian angel to come close to you. Feel your angel's wings enfold you with love as you relax completely, knowing that you are totally protected.

STEP 3

Ask your angel for any help that you need. Be specific if you wish. Angels will help you with any task, from the smallest niggling problem to the biggest burdens you may carry.

STEP 4

Feel the love surrounding you. Breathe in all the love you feel: you deserve all the love you need.

STEP 5

Before you open your eyes thank your guardian angel for its grace. The more often you meet like this the closer you will become: some people actually get to see their angel.

If you want angels to become part of your everyday life then just focus on them. The more you think about them the closer they will come.

3 Expecting a Miracle

Miracles are love in action.

Miracles are love in action and if you don't believe in them they will never happen to you. We can attract miracles into our lives but only if we truly believe they are possible. Forget about not *really* allowing yourself to believe in case you are disappointed. Fear of disappointment will stand in your way for ever! You are disappointed anyway – what have you got to lose?

Expect a miracle for a week. Wholeheartedly believe that one will happen and *keep trusting*. The miracle might not be the one you were expecting but I can assure you that *something amazing* will happen. Belief is the most powerful magic of all.

You are never alone as you walk through your life. Close at hand (and even closer than that) is an angelic host just waiting to be called upon. Why struggle through your problems alone when all love and assistance is yours for the asking? Suspend your disbelief in the world of spirit: what have you got to lose? Invite the angels into your life and everything will change. You will feel uplifted, spiritually stronger and altogether more confident in your day-to-day affairs. Choose to live with the angels and turn an ordinary life into a magical experience!

KEY POWER POINTS

These key points are here to remind you of why you are doing your *Receiving Angelic Blessings* workouts. Refer to this list for constant encouragement and support. Reclaim the power that is yours!

1   Angels are right beside us all the time, just waiting to help. We only have to ask.
2   We can receive the precious gifts of peace, love and harmony by fulfilling our divine connection.
3   If you only knew how much help the angelic world can give you, you would never feel frightened and alone again.

133

4   Open your heart, suspend your disbelief and you will see what the universe can offer you.

5   You deserve all the love, support and help that you need.

6   The more you focus on angels the closer they will come.

7   Miracles are love in action.

8   Wholeheartedly expect a miracle and something amazing will happen – just believe.

9   Belief is the most powerful magic in the universe.

10   Your angel always loves you (warts and all).

19 Bouncing Back

When the going gets rough the tough just get tougher.

- When your mind is full of 'if only's.
- When you feel that you have been victimized.
- When the going gets so tough that you feel you can't cope a moment longer.
- When you feel that you have been chosen to experience bad luck or that you are being punished for something.
- When you can't stop feeling sorry for yourself.
- If you feel that your world has fallen apart.
- Whenever you lose faith in people and the universe.
- When it's hard to find anything to be happy about.

An important relationship ends badly; you suffer a health problem; a loved one is in trouble; you don't get that coveted job; you suffer a bereavement … I'm sure that you can add your own major setbacks to this list of examples. Anything that happens that blows your world apart will qualify.

Terrible things *do* happen to people and there's nothing unusual about having to face a big setback. The important question is not 'why has this happened to me?' but 'how can I learn to bounce back from adversity?'

When we face a devastating problem we are at our lowest and may experience feelings such as:

Loss of faith in ourselves and others. *How could they do this to me?*

Low levels of confidence. *How can I cope?*
Feeling sorry for ourselves. *Why has this happened to me? Do I deserve this? Am I being punished?*

Know that you are a strong and resilient woman: you have all the skills to deal creatively with any setback you encounter. You will survive this!

HOW TO BOUNCE BACK

These workouts offer guidelines to help you to pick up the pieces when you are feeling devastated by adversity. Workout 1 will look at how you have dealt with disappointments in the past and show you how you can learn from these occasions. Workout 2 looks at a variety of survival tactics to help you to cope and Workout 3 shows how to look forward to a new future rather than worrying about what might have been.

1 Changing Your Management Strategies

Think back to some past disappointments and setbacks. Make a list of them and then look at them one at a time and analyze how you coped at the time. Could you have got through the bad times quicker if you had used different tactics?

For example, did you keep talking about the problem with your family and friends? Sometimes this helps, but only up to a point. Continual discharge about your problems to those around you can just serve to keep your worries alive and in the present. Have you ever heard someone going on and on about their latest operation and revelling in the pain? This method does not help them get better.

Did you really need to look at some deep feelings? Would professional counselling have helped? Did you become very negative? Did you experience feelings: 'I feel ill, I can't imagine that I'll ever feel well again'; 'he's walked out on me and I know I'll never be happy again'; 'I didn't get that great job and I am just not interested in working anywhere else'?

Of course you will feel negative when the event happens, this is quite natural. But life goes on and if you can only allow the seeds of hope into your mind you can speed up your healing process. Everything changes, although this is so hard to believe when things are looking black. Often we can look back at events in the past and think that perhaps that particular disappointment was all for the best. So you didn't get that job but maybe as a result you changed your career path. Was that gorgeous man who walked out on you really that terrific? Perhaps you are in a new and better relationship now. Learn what you can from every setback and always remember that as one door closes another opens. When you have overcome the initial shock of your disappointment, employ some new coping strategies and keep looking for that newly opening door – when you spot it *go through it* and then you will know that you have bounced back!

2 Using Survival Tactics

- Accept the reality of what has happened to you.
- Don't allow your mind to keep replaying the event. Wondering what you did wrong and dwelling on 'if onlys' will not give you anything except sleepless nights.
- Visualize yourself coping well and moving on into your new future.

- Try to stop blaming yourself or anyone else for your misfortune: bad things happen.
- Don't compare yourself with anyone else, either with someone who has 'all the luck' or with that 'poor soul' who is so much worse off than you. You can't compare levels of pain and there is nothing to be gained from it. Acknowledge and feel your pain and then start moving out of it.
- Make the following affirmation:

I am a strong and powerful woman and I know how to bounce back.

Say this to yourself every time you remember. Fill your mind with empowering thoughts and you will feel stronger and more effective.
- Realize that you will have dark times when you feel that you will never get over your pain, and remember that eventually you will. You will survive this!
- The darkest light is just before the dawn.

3 Looking Forward

When we suffer disappointments and difficulties we tend to focus on 'what might have been' rather than what is.

Do you recognize any of these thoughts?

- If only I hadn't done that.
- I wish I had said something else.
- I should have behaved differently.
- I regret doing that.
- If only I could do it all over again.

They often come to us in the small hours of the morning when we have time to ponder our difficulties. We have all lain there in the dark, worrying and blaming ourselves for what has happened and wishing we had done something different.

We can all look back and regret our actions but *we cannot change the past*, and if we continue to agonize over what we should and shouldn't have done we will remain stuck in the past. Stop blaming yourself (or anyone else), let go of guilt and bounce back to create a bright, new, positive future.

Life is full of setbacks and the only way to survive them is to learn how to lift yourself up from rock bottom and bounce back with even more stamina. Women have amazing levels of endurance, perseverance and emotional strength (I'm sure that you will agree). Remember this when you are feeling weak and disempowered in the face of adversity. You can deal with whatever life throws at you. Take strength from past successes. You are a survivor!

KEY POWER POINTS

These key points are here to remind you of why you are doing your *Bouncing Back* workouts. Refer to this list for constant encouragement and support. Reclaim the power that is yours!

1   When the going gets rough the tough just get tougher, and that means you!
2   The big question is not 'why has this happened to me?', but 'how can I learn to bounce back from adversity?'
3   You are a strong and resilient woman with all the skills you need to deal creatively with any setback you encounter. You will survive this!

139

4   Don't keep talking about your problems to friends and family. If you need to look at important issues seek professional help.

5   Keep looking for that newly opening door and when you see it *go through it!*

6   Visualize yourself coping well and moving into your bright new future.

7   Don't compare your situation with anyone else's; this won't do anything to help you.

8   Keep making this affirmation: *I am a strong and powerful woman and I know how to bounce back.* Repeat this as often as necessary and then you will start to believe it.

9   You cannot change the past but you can change the way you look at the past.

10   The darkest light is just before the dawn (truly!).

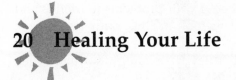

20 Healing Your Life

When we really love ourselves, everything in our life works.
Louise Hay

- When everything in your life seems to be going wrong.
- When you don't like yourself and are low in confidence.
- Whenever any part of your life feels out of balance.
- If you are physically ill.
- If you are emotionally upset.
- If you feel spiritually disconnected.
- If you are thinking and speaking negatively.
- When you feel out of control.

'To heal' literally means 'to make whole', and every time we have a problem, whether it's *physical, emotional, mental* or *spiritual,* we are being shown a place where we need to heal ourselves (make ourselves whole). Figure 4 shows how these four interrelated aspects of ourselves come together to create our whole self.

When we *are* balanced, our energy is flowing freely and we feel wonderful: our mental, physical, emotional and spiritual energies are in harmony and we are 'at ease'. If, for some reason, there is a block in the circuit, and this can be in any one or more of the levels, then we become out of balance and this affects every part of our being. When we are out of balance we are dis-eased (not at ease) with ourselves and eventually we become diseased in some way.

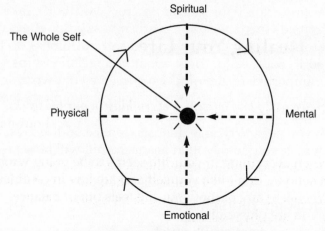

Figure 4. The Whole Self

Your own healing ultimately rests with you. Only you can know the delicate interplay between your energies; only you know what you need for your own mental, emotional, spiritual and physical health; only you can choose to create health and balance in your life: only you can heal your life!

HOW TO HEAL YOUR LIFE

The first workout demonstrates how you can take charge of your own healing *whatever* the problem might be. Workouts 2–4 suggest ways to help you to balance your mind, body, spirit and emotions. You will have to answer some searching questions here, so be prepared!

1 Taking Charge of Your Own Healing

However ill you feel, whatever psychological problems you face, you can still be in charge of your own healing. If you have a physical condition find out all you can about it –

don't just expect the doctor to 'sort you out'. Take the prescribed medicine but also investigate alternative approaches. Look at your lifestyle and nutrition – do they support good health? How about your relationships – are they supportive or stressful? Do you love your work or is it winding you up? Look beyond a single symptom, look at the *whole* picture of your life.

Do you need to change things to reduce undue stress and tension? If you do then that headache pill will never work, there are deeper issues here.

2 Checking Yourself Out

RUN SOME BODY CHECKS THROUGHOUT THE DAY
Whenever you become aware of your own changes in mood (eg emotional highs and lows, feelings of calm or stress, confidence or lack of it) check your physical reaction. Notice any changes in energy levels, posture or physical symptoms. How does your body feel when you are high in confidence? Do you walk differently? What happens when things go wrong? How does your body feel? We all react differently, so take some time to think about the way your own body responds to different emotional states. Your body talks to you in many different ways, listen to it and respond to its needs.

CONSIDER YOUR BELIEFS AND EMOTIONS
Our bodies are a reflection of our inner states. Ask yourself what sort of beliefs have created your own mental patterns? Are they supportive and nurturing or negative and depressing? Are your emotions allowed expression and release or do they sit inside you attracting angry and resentful thoughts?

143

ASK YOURSELF IF YOU REALLY WANT TO BE HEALTHY

This is an important question. Sometimes there may be 'something in it' for us to be sick. We can use illness as a way to avoid responsibilities and/or we can use our sickness as a way to say 'no' in a situation where we find it difficult to assert ourselves. Perhaps we are not good at nurturing ourselves and our illness means that we will get cared for by someone else.

3 Loving Yourself to Heal Your Life

The more you love yourself the more balanced your life will be and so you will feel more 'whole'. When we can trust ourselves enough to tap into our intuition we can start to care for and nurture ourselves. Once we respect ourselves we find it easier to be assertive and to communicate our needs to the people in our life. When we are saying what we mean our body responds to that emotional honesty and our limiting behaviour patterns will start to change. When you are ill, your body is trying to tell you something. Rest and listen to its messages. Why are you ill? What sort of health are your thoughts and behaviour attracting to you? Love and appreciate yourself to heal your life.

4 Making Positive Affirmations for Health

Make any of these affirmations as often as you can. Write them, say them, sing them, *live them!* Surround yourself with love and healing consciousness and feel your energy respond.

AFFIRMATIONS:
I deserve vibrant health.
I love my body.

I can heal myself.
I listen and respond to my body's messages.
I create harmony and balance within my body.
The universal life force flows easily through me.
I trust my inner messages.
It is safe to be well.
I am ready to be well, now.
I love and value myself.

For a comprehensive list of illnesses, corresponding thought patterns and healing affirmations see Louise Hay's amazing book, *You Can Heal Your Life.*

The secret of good health is simple:

Love Yourself
Forgive Yourself
Release All Blame
Release All Negative Thought Patterns
Express Your Needs
Take Care of Your Body
Trust Your Intuition

You are a valuable and worthy person who deserves to be healthy.

KEY POWER POINTS

These key points are here to remind you of why you are doing your *Healing Your Life* workouts. Refer to this list for constant encouragement and support. Reclaim the power that is yours!

Healing

1   Every time you have a problem, whether it's physical, emotional, mental or spiritual, you are being shown a place where you need to heal yourself.

2   Only you can choose to create health and balance in your life: only you can choose to heal your life!

3   Take charge of your own healing: look beyond a single symptom, look at the *whole* picture of your life.

4   Look at your lifestyle and nutrition. Do they support good health?

5   Your body talks to you in many different ways. Listen to it and respond to its needs.

5   Our bodies are reflections of our inner states: keep a check on your thoughts and unexpressed feelings.

6   Love and appreciate yourself to heal your life.

7   Make positive affirmations for good health. Surround yourself with love and healing consciousness and feel your energy respond.

8   You deserve vibrant health.

9   Forgive yourself and everyone else; you will feel lighter and brighter.

10   It is safe to be well!